PEOPLE & PLACES
IN SANCREED PARISH

by
Jim Hosking
'Ystorer Trevow' (Historian of Villages)

GW00480690

Cover Picture: Sancreed Church & War Memorial

Other Books

1970 - To America and Back 1811

1978 - This is our life (a book of verse)

1981 - Methodism in St Buryan

1985 - Camping tales of Tower Farm

2002 - People, Places & Past Events in St Buryan

2005 - People & Places in Paul Parish

Published by J.M. Hosking 2008

Pentreath, 9 Tredarvah Drive, Penzance, Cornwall UK TR18 4SU

Email: jimtredarvah@tiscali.co.uk

ISBN 978-0-9501296-7-9   © J.M. Hosking

Printed by Headland Printers Ltd., Penzance, Cornwall

FOREWORD

I am honoured to have been asked to provide a foreword to this latest publication by the well-named Cornish Bard 'Ystorer Trevow', the 'Historian of Villages'. This volume on Sancreed is yet another invaluable contribution to the chronicling of West Cornwall's rich history, and records numerous fascinating facets of the past within this extensive parish.

The area's history is, of course, intrinsically bound up with the lives and personalities of its inhabitants, and this is what comes across so delightfully in Jim Hosking's books. Dry facts are well preserved through the excellent auspices of institutions such as the Cornwall Records Office and the Cornwall Centre, Redruth, but the telling of remembered tales of long-dead forebears is all too often lost. What makes Jim's publications unique is the way in which he captures the fast vanishing memories of local places, using first-person narratives to bring the stories alive.

As ever, Jim Hosking has been astonishingly diligent in his research for this book, clocking up many road miles weaving through the meandering lanes of Sancreed, and doubtless using almost equal miles of tape recording people's stories. To this he adds scholarly research from written sources, and uses his skills as a narrator to communicate an utterly infectious interest in the lives of others, past and present.

Those whose families or properties are featured in this book (and I'll confess the selfish interest of being one of the lucky inhabitants of Sancreed parish) will need no further inducement to buy a copy, but will be richly rewarded by its contents. Even if you have never been to Sancreed, however, the many and varied human stories contained in this publication are of universal interest, offering a source of enjoyment to return to again and again.

Alison Bevan Oct 2008
Director,
Penlee House Gallery & Museum, Penzance

CONTENTS

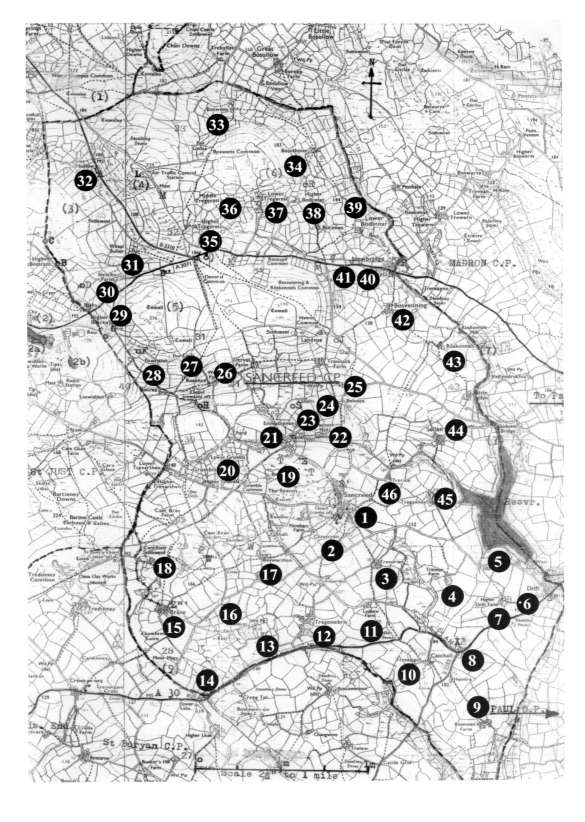

MAP INDEX

INTRODUCTION:

King Athelstan and his army spent the night in St Buryan. The Spaniards burnt Paul Church. What exciting events befell Sancreed?

This book takes you on a tour clock wise around almost all the farms of Sancreed with many stories by Sancreed people including 5 nonagenarians. You will have some surprises!

Although the sea can be seen from much of the parish, Sancreed, is the only one on the Lands End peninsula without a coastline. It is surrounded by the parishes of Paul, St Buryan, St Just, Pendeen, & Madron.

It incorporates an introduction to Sancreed village, Drift, and Newbridge.

SANCREED

"What is the mystery, who can tell, Of Sancreed's ancient holy well
Or when, or why, St Credan came, and how my parish bears his name?
Why, everywhere the varied traces, of time-lost prehistoric races,
The beehive-huts, menhirs, holed stones, fragments of urns and calcined bones.
Then whilst St Credan had his cell, and baptised at his Holy Well,
St Euney's Chapel, sacred spring, held healing powers for everything.
Historians, still at a loss to classify each Christian cross,
On most the well accepted sign, while others bear a strange design.
The sites of early games are seen, one Churchway field 'The Bowling Green',
Archers, perhaps, from days of woad, still are recalled along 'Butts Road'
Tin streamers too, have left their trace, though almost a forgotten race,
The waste from mines can still be found from shafts and levels underground.
'God's Acre!' tells its simple story, twixt rural folk and 'deeds of glory',
Great artists in its peace abide, their magic brushes laid aside.
This 'island' parish has no coast, an inland 'gem stone', I love most,
In Penwith, bounded by the sea, makes it unique, at least to me.
So Credan, from the Emerald Isle, dwelt in this parish for a while,
To some a Saint of minor fame, yet Sancreed proudly bears his name."

by Bill Watters

CHAPTER 1

SANCREED VILLAGE AREA

Sancreed Church

One can't imagine for a moment that this lovely church was always so hidden away, so that coming around the corner you see it, amongst the trees, waiting to be discovered by each new passer-by. Raised on its surrounding burial ground, in the lee of the Beacon beyond, it has fascinated many who feel at peace there. Amongst others were some of the artists of the now famous Newlyn School, who came over from Trewarveneth in Newlyn to worship and to later lie in the Churchyard.

Inside the building is part of an old rood screen, of which Sedding says: "I know of no finer specimen elsewhere in the country. Like so much old Cornish work it is more than local; it is purely parochial."

Kelly's Directory 1893 "The church of San Creed (or Sancta Creda) is a building of granite, chiefly in the late 15th century style, consisting of chancel, nave, aisles, transepts, south porch and an embattled western tower with pinnacles containing 3 bells: the rood stairs, piscina and stoup remain: some carving on the rood screen is possibly Spanish: the restoration of the church, begun in 1881, under the direction of Mr. J. D. Sedding, architect, was completed in 1891 at a cost of £2,350: the church has been new roofed,

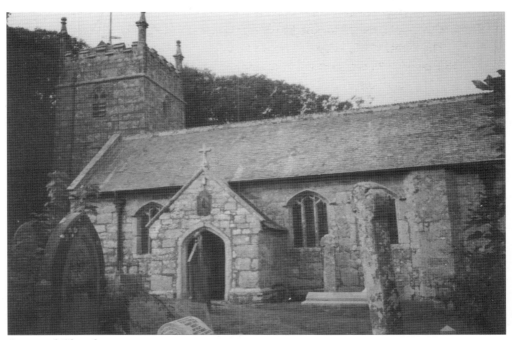

Sancreed Church.

9

refloored and reseated with carved oak benches affording 240 sittings, and internal fittings are still (1893) being added: during the restoration the remains of a Norman font were found".

Sancreed Church.

The Church in Sancreed has served the parish for centuries and a possible candidate for its patron saint is said to be St Credan, son of Illaidan. The story goes that this young man accidentally killed his father and to show his great remorse punished himself by living his life as a lowly hogsherd. The exemplary life St Credan led caused him to be recognised as a saint and his Feast is kept on the first Sunday in June. The advowson of Sancreed appears to have been attached originally to the Manor of Bosvenning, held by the Earl of Gloucester. It was transferred in 1182 by the latter to the Church of St James, Bristol, a priory or cell of the Abbey of Tewkesbury, whence it passed, in 1243, to the Dean and Chapter of Exeter, who continued to exercise the right of patronage until 1889, when it was vested in the Dean and Chapter of the newly formed diocese of Truro.

Although the church is referred to in documents of the twelfth century, the first incumbent of whom there is any record is Thomas Durant, instituted on September 28, 1289.

A spire?

The west tower, massive and low, of two stages, was probably, it has been said, designed in the first place for a spire. The bells are three in number-a treble of 1759, a tenor of 1774 and a second tenor of 1882.

Fish and leprosy?

An interesting glimpse both of social conditions and of the relative value of money in the days of the first rector, is afforded by the will of Bishop Bytton of Exeter (1291-1307). The Bishop, in whose diocese the parish then was, left legacies to no less than twenty-three leper hospitals in Cornwall, among them one of sixpence to that of Sancto Sancredo.

Many thought that eating fish was the cause of the many lepers in West Cornwall, Paul, Sancreed, Madron & St Ives, but the more likely reason was that any who contracted leprosy on board ship were put ashore at the first convenient port.

From John Wesley's diary

SUNDAY, SEPTEMBER 4TH.1768 Wesley wrote, *"I went to Sancreed church, where I heard an excellent sermon. Between one and two I confirmed it by explaining that happy religion which our Lord describes in the Eight Beatitudes."*

The vicar, Rev. Edward Hobbes, was at Sancreed until his death in 1772. He was a man of exemplary character.

A convenient seat and other tales
On Feast Sunday in 1667 the parishioners pulled John Smythe, their Vicar, from the pulpit and took action against him in the Bishop's Court for making jokes at their expense in his sermons. "Others are pastors of their flock" he said "but I am a herdsman of a company of swine!"

In July 1671, Bishop Sparrow's report on the Church at Sancreed revealed that some parishioners were 'up in arms' about precedence in church sittings.
A man called John Adams "of mean estate and fortune" had actually seated himself higher-up than "those who are of the Twelve of the parish and their wives" so that Francis Lanyon, whose wife was a niece of Colonel Godolphin of Trewarveneth, was without a convenient seat.

Highwayman
The parson's advice was often sought on secular matters. On one occasion in the middle of the last century, an old road-mender, who was also a local preacher on the 'chapel plan', came to the vicar of his parish to consult him about a census form, which he had received. "There's seems a purty lot of questions to answer, sir," he remarked. "And there's one which do ask what my occupation is. Do'ee thinks I had best put down 'Local Preacher and Highwayman'?"

Betty the Barrel
There was at quaint old character of St Just nicknamed 'Betty the Barrel'. Learning on one occasion of the arrival of a new parson at Sancreed, Betty made her way there on the following Sunday to hear him preach. On his return to the vicarage after service, the parson was surprised to find the old lady wandering up and down in his garden. Thinking she must be either deranged in her mind or there for no good purpose, he went out and asked her what she wanted. 'Oh, my dear sir,' was the reply, 'I've heerd one blessed sarmon this morning and I'm going to stay and hear another before I go home.' The guileless parson, imagining the old humbug to be sincere, brought her in and gave her a good dinner, assuring her that she was welcome to dine there any Sunday she wished. Some time after this the vicar himself called one day at Betty's house, where the old woman happened to be seated over a cup of tea and a nice bit of saffron cake. Catching sight of her visitor she had just time to hide the cake and substitute with a dry crust before he entered the room. At the sight of this poor-looking fare the parson naturally asked: 'Is that the best you've got to eat, Betty?' 'Oh, my dear sir,' came her humble reply, 'I've got Christ with my crust' a pious statement, for which she was promptly rewarded with the gift of a crown.

Extracts from *Yesterday* by His Honour J W Scobell Armstrong C.B.E
"Reverend George Pender Scobell, my great great grandfather, was vicar of Sancreed and of St Just, two livings not far from Land's End. This family lived at Sancreed and

when driving from the vicarage there to the service at St Just used, I am told, to relieve the tedium of the drive by playing whist in the wagonette. The vicar was a gentle, kindly man.

John Opie artist

When one day there arrived at the door a young strolling artist who wanted to paint his portrait, he offered him hospitality at the vicarage and commissioned him to paint the whole family one after another for a guinea apiece. The young painter in question was John Opie, the boy whom Dr. Wolcot of Truro had extracted from a sawpit, who a year or two later was acclaimed in London as 'the Cornish wonder'. He was presented to George III and his Queen, who bought two of his pictures and gave him a commission. John Opie painted more than 750 pictures, died aged 46, and was buried in St Pauls Cathedral".

At the vicar's bedside

Phyllis Jilbert, nee Hosking: "I used to go to church every Sunday, and when the vicar the Rev Stona was ill and in the bed, he sent word he wanted to see me. I didn't know what to say to him. I was only a young girl. He said, 'I strain my ears to hear the singing every Sunday night'. I was with him just a day or two before he died. Our family were often the only children at the church." Rev John Stona was vicar at Sancreed for 45 years until 1945.

Grave of Stanhope Forbes.

In Sancreed Churchyard are graves of famous artists

In Sancreed Churchyard you may see the graves of Stanhope A Forbes, his first wife, Elizabeth Adela, (nee Armstrong), his second wife, Maud Clayton and also his mother-in-law, Frances Armstrong. Inside the church is a plaque in memory of his son WILLIAM ALEXANDER STANHOPE FORBES, killed leading his Platoon on the Somme battlefield in France. 3rd.Sept. 1916.

Also buried at Sancreed are artists Florence Munnings (AJ Munning's first wife); Thomas, Caroline and Phyllis Gotch; George Sherwood Hunter; Henry Meynell Rheam; Peter and Jill Gamier; and Kate Westrup.

Sancreed Holy Well

Sancreed Holy Well, near to Sancreed Church, known locally as Crone Well, is underground and close to the remains of a small chapel. The Rev A. Lane-Davies, in his book "Holy Wells of Cornwall", writes about Sancreed Well, *"The spot always seems to me to possess a greater air of mystery and sanctity than any other in Cornwall."* There is a 'cloutie' tree by the well where fragments of garments worn by those with an ailment were tied. As the fragment of material (cloutie) deteriorated, so the ailment was meant to have lessened.

Sancreed Holy Well.

Bird in Hand, Sancreed & the hurlers

From *Hearthside Stories* by William Bottrell "The last inn sign had the words *'A bird in hand is better far than two that in the bushes are'* printed beneath a fluttering bird, its legs grasped by a hand.

The meaning of this goes back to when 'regulars' would put their drinks 'on the slate', to be settled when funds allowed. However, on 'high days and holidays' only cash paying customers were served as at busy times staff could not 'stay to use the chalk'.

Hurling and wrestling were common sports amongst young Sancreed men, fit from working in the mines or on the land and used to walking miles each day.

Many parishes had hurling teams that would compete against each other, the two teams of up to 60 persons vying to catch and retain a thrown, silver covered, wooden ball and carry it over 3 or 4 miles to an agreed 'winning post' where the local gentry would award substantial prizes to the winner. Teams must have suffered many casualties battling their speedy way over extremely rough terrain, through bogs and streams, over hills and moorland, to say nothing of negotiating mine workings!

One farmer's son, soon to be married, celebrated his victory at hurling perhaps a little too well. On a night when bonfires were lit on the beacons across Cornwall, a sudden thick mist descended and he found himself going round in circles trying to reach the singing and dancing he could hear close by on Sancreed Beacon. At the foot of Beacon Hill, which was shunned by locals after dark, he realised he had become 'piskey led'. He was found at first light, lying insensible and badly hurt by the spurs he had won as a trophy at hurling, which had penetrated his flesh from his inside pocket where he had placed them. He did marry but led a more sober life thereafter!"

Probably only the older residents of the parish are aware that the Glebe Farmhouse was actually the Bird-in-Hand inn until 1880. Now a private dwelling, it was built in the first years of Queen Victoria's reign. However, there was an inn on the same site as far back as the 1600's, across the road from the Parish Church.

The inn, part of a larger tenancy including a farm, was the property of the Ecclesiastical Commissioners, supervised by the vicar. When a customer was drowned in a well there, the vicar felt responsible and closed the pub.

The "Bird in Hand" pub by Kathleen Hawke
Wrestling Matches, donkey races, rattling chains & the landlady.

In the days when the production of tin was in full swing in the locality, the life of Sancreed's prosperous community circled round the Bird-in-Hand.

Caer Bran, Beacon, Wheal Argus, West Ding Dong, and Carney Barges were the names of tin mines worked in Sancreed, which was then a noted place.

The population of the parish was at its highest in 1851 when it was 1,398. In 1901 it had fallen to 784. With the decline of tin-mining and the closing of the inn the village became being used for cattle sheds. There are still a few reminders of the pastimes which the miners indulged in at Bird-in-Hand Farm when "out of core" or on "Mazed Monday". This was the Monday after the men received their pay, and was a time for great jollification.

A three-acre field was used for sports, which consisted chiefly of wrestling matches and donkey races. A lot of miners used donkeys for transport and in the races no one was allowed to ride his own donkey, the last donkey winning the prize. It was considered good sport but not from the donkey's point of view, as the poor things must often have suffered from exhaustion. The field above, used for the sports, is still called the Bowling Green. It is on a higher level and was used as a grandstand when sports were in progress below.

South of the church is Park Down field. The latter had a pool near it where the cows drank, known as Devil's Pool, and if you ran round it seven times you would hear the devil rattling his chains. It has now been filled in.

Near the Bird-in-Hand there is a small enclosure, which goes by the name of Kilalley, which of course is a corruption of Keel (Skittle) Alley. A building attached at an angle on the right of the inn was formerly used as a shop by a local butcher.

There was a story told of a former landlord's wife who became too fond of intoxicating liquor. During his absence her husband used to take the precaution to lock the doors of the cellar and main bar. One day, however, he forgot to fasten the bar window and as it opened

upwards the lady managed to get inside. Unfortunately when she was making her exit the window dropped, and she remained suspended until someone came along and released her. The old hepping-stock, the village pump, and the granite trough where the horses used to drink are decidedly quieter. I can remember about forty derelict houses in the parish, some of which still remain as relics of an almost forgotten era."

The Bird in Hand.

James Stevens *"London is not in my district!"*

In 1897 at the age of fifty, James Stevens Snr. with his wife Honor, came from Zennor to live at Sancreed in 1897 and took over the farm then known as Glebe Farm, at that time property of the church. He was a very well known and respected farmer, a popular figure involved in the church, cricket, parish, and district. He kept a diary over a period of 20 years. *A Cornish Farmer's Diary* has been edited by P.A.S.Pool. James had a saying *"Farm as if you were going to live for ever and live as if you were going to die tonight"* and the diary shows that he both farmed and lived accordingly.

Rev. Stona was installed at Sancreed in 1900. On arrival he antagonised the choir and churchwardens by changing long-standing practices. He could not maintain good relations or mutual tolerance with the Methodists. There was bitter discord about educational matters in the schools. The vicar's hayrick was set on fire in1903. In 1904 James Stevens was made People's Warden and perhaps his early Methodist upbringing helped him in sorting out the problems he had to face. In a poem he wrote in 1903
I Love The Church

> *I love the Church, I love her ways, I love her songs, I love her lays,*
>
> *I love her rules, I love her guides, I'll stick to her, whate'er betides.*

He was devout and hard-working both on the farm and for the village communities in which he spent his life.

James Stevens once went as far as Truro where he had been summoned to serve on a jury. That was as far as he had travelled from Lands End. When London was mentioned he said, "London is not my district". He retired from farming in1914 and died in 1918.

James Stevens the younger

By 1892 James Stevens the younger had left school and was helping his father on the farm and sometimes working for other farmers.

From childhood he had shown musical talent and in verses written many years later he recalled singing in the Zennor Church Choir from the singers' gallery, removed in 1890:-

> *I joined the Choir when I was nine and sang up in the gallery*
>
> *With other boys all in a line, we never sang for salary.*

Handed down Memories

James Stevens's grandaughters Gwen and Kathleen lived at Glebe after he and Honor, his wife, had retired to Little Grumbla when their parents exchanged homes.

They loved dressing up with old clothes found in the attic and said that their Mother Esther was never too busy to shriek with laughter or be impressed however busy she was.

On the rare occasions when the famous artist Stanhope Forbes attended Morning Service at Sancreed from his home at Trewarveneth, Paul, Kathleen Stevens (later to become the Cornish Bard Kathleen Hawke) would eagerly offer to hold his horse for sixpence and go to church herself in the evening. I believe he also gave her painting lessons and was a very kind gentleman.

James took over Glebe Farm from his father first as a tenant and later owner and retired in 1944.

In 1946 he composed the following, which is shortened:

Sancreed in Script   by James Stevens the Younger

This is Sancreed and tho' we've no sea coast,
we've other attractions of which we can boast
The view from our hilltops is one of the best our rivers and valleys can rival the rest.
The Church with· its tower almost hid by the tree is open for all
to come as they please;
Rich carvings in oak adorn the inside and tablets in memory of those who have died.
A sundial fixed just o'er the porch gate keeps time for worshippers
whether early or late;
A silent time-keeper for those who are dead;
and they who are christened and those who are wed.

Major Saddler

In 1944 Major A. Sadler bought *The Glebe* and renamed it *The Bird In Hand* again. He rode around in an American Jeep and wore shorts all the year round. He was president of the Western Area Agricultural Competitions in 1945 at Trenuggo. He stayed at The *Bird in Hand* until March 1958.

Norman Hosking

On March 27th 1958 Norman Hosking with his father and mother moved to Glebe Farm from Boskenna Home Farm, St Buryan. Norman lived and worked there until October 2003 when he and his wife Marion retired to Penzance.

While living at Glebe he grew all kinds of vegetables and exhibited them in horticultural shows from Sancreed to Scotland.

Prince Charles congratulates Norman Hosking on his prize winning 12ft carrot.

With potatoes he became the Scottish champion in 1997 and UK champion in 1999. From Dundee to Pembroke, from the Royal Horticultural Society, London, to the Royal Agricultural Society, he has won over 1,000 1st and 2nd prizes in competitions in the most prestigious events in the English, Scottish, and Welsh calendar. Norman is a champion among champions in the potato exhibiting world.

He has been featured on TV and is in the Guinness Book of World Records for 525 different varieties of potatoes.

Norman's wife Marion (nee Nicholls) lived and went to school at Newbridge as a child. She moved to Pendeen in her teens. The couple have one son Julian.

Marion's story.

Norman sold vegetables at the door and found a ready market for them "We were selling vegetables one day when a coach arrived with people who had come to look at the Church. Norman had new potatoes for sale and they all queued up for them. While I was weighing and selling them Norman was digging them and the coach driver was going up and down from the field keeping me supplied!

The film *To the Lighthouse* was partly filmed in Sancreed using the house of John Miller the artist. They used our yard for the canteen. Toyah Wilcox also came and Robert Fripp with his band. Harry Secombe filmed some of *Highway* with John Miller.

I always loved Glebe house and was amazed that I came to work and live there for 33 years.

When I met Norman it was a while before I realized he was living in the house I had always loved so much."

John Miller 1931- 2002
Notes from his book *Leave tomorrow behind*

Encouraged by his father John Miller painted in watercolour from an early age and spent the long summer holidays sketching in Sussex and Surrey. He helped fund his sketching expeditions by painting pictures of public houses and offering these to the landlords. He was called up for National Service on his eighteenth birthday. The next year he was commissioned. He was sent to Malta, and wrote, "It was an entirely new experience of light and colour."

When he spent some time in hospital he painted there. When in Malta he became involved in

John Miller in his studio.

the theatre. After military service he worked for church architects, attended evening classes at the Regent School of Architecture. He painted portraits at the weekends and stayed at Nanquidno with friends of his parents. He had come to Cornwall to measure the rood screen in St Buryan Church for an architectural exam. In St Buryan he called on Ashley Thomas the local carpenter and undertaker to borrow a ladder.

The late **John Miller** "Mr Thomas selected a suitable ladder then took me into his house where he asked his wife if there was any chance of an extra pasty for lunch. That was my first real Cornish pasty and it was delicious. It was also my first experience of Cornish hospitality, which confirmed my growing desire to return one day to live out the rest of my life in this magical land.

Sancreed House was built as a vicarage in 1830. It had become redundant two years before the previous owners bought it. The last vicar was Paul Nichols, brother of Beverley whom we had met in the Richmond days. It is as though destiny first brought me to Sancreed and that, there, in the heart of the Penwith peninsula I found a meaning in my life. David and Jane Cornwell (John le Carré) lived there before buying Tregiffian. David wrote *'The Native and Sentimental Lover'* at Sancreed. We had known one another before the success of *'The Spy Who Came in from the Cold'* and our friendship was sealed when they lived at Sancreed. I am a godfather to their son Michael. I rejoice that there is so much more life to be shared here - and so much more to paint. I can only celebrate all that fills me with joy and wonder by painting in my own way. I cannot describe the process very well nor can I justify it, which is possibly why I am shy about openings.

I would like to think that it has something to do with what a neighbouring farmer said to me when we met on a day my painting was in the doldrums. 'Well now John, are you putting enough love into your work? You see, I couldn't tend those cows properly if I didn't love them. I couldn't build up that stone hedge if I didn't love the stones, nor could I 'teel' that field of potatoes if I didn't love the earth and the plants - and, in truth, the whole of God's creation".

Michael Truscott

In the attractive white and terracotta vicarage next door was a studio and pottery where John's friend Michael Truscott made and sold jugs and bowls with a beautiful matt blue finish.

Sancreed School

The last Sancreed School opened in 1864 and closed in 1983.

There were other schools in Sancreed before this. (A Mary Ann Read of Free School House, Church Town died age 49 in November 1831).

In 1864 the new headmaster, Edward Heywood, came from Chester Training College. There were 40 pupils.

The school log book showed there were many absentees: - market day, tilling potatoes, whooping cough, fair in Penzance. In 1869 it was reported that the school had been opened in the past year 442 times. Only 6 scholars have been present more than 400 times. The H.M. inspector reported the religious exams, the spelling and arithmetic not so good but reading, writing, and needlework were very good.

In 1880 the inspector reported that the answering was partial and wanting in intelligence but the following are worthy of special commendation - J H Pengelly, P Pengelly, Ann Semmens also commended.

In 1907 the vicar, Rev. Stona, was defendant on a charge of libel or slander by Mr & Mrs Ireland, former teachers at Sancreed School, who were claiming £1250 damages.

Schooldays – as told by Richard Norman Hosking from Boswarthan

"There were two teachers at Sancreed School when I started in 1924. Walking from Sellan farm cottage we were about one mile from school. My brother, three years older than me, took me. When he started he had been taken on the back of our father's motorbike. The teacher of the infants was Miss Williams. I think I was rather afraid of her, the only thing I remember of that time on one of my first days at school was my brother eating my dinner as well as his own and an older boy having to take me home to dinner as my brother had forgotten I was there!

My next move was to the big room with the master, Mr Martin. He was tall, with grey hair and a moustache. He sat at his desk twiddling his moustache or walked up and down the classroom with the cane in his hand. The infants' room, or little room as we called it, was separated by a wood and glass partition, which could be folded back for any occasion.

The top class desks had lids and inside held all their books, seven children sat on a form, which was attached to the desk. There were three rows of these, then three rows with just a plain top desk and form and another three rows similar.

Playtime games had their crazes, whipping tops, marbles, cars or motorbikes, later yoyos. In summer there was 'fox and hounds', cricket and looking for birds nests. Girls would be playing skipping and the 'Farmer's in his den' and tig or tag was a regular for both boys and girls. Once hoops were the craze, the boys had iron hoops which we truckled to school and the girls had wooden hoops. There was always the collecting of cigarette cards and swapping.

Sancreed School about 1948.
Back Row from left: Mr. Gelling, Owen Williams, John Lawrey, Dennis Drew, Eric Rowe, George Lawry, Godfrey Drew, ? Kessell, Russell Giles, David Taylor, Arthur Hosking, Miss May (teacher).
Row 2: Joyce Elliot, Diana Armour, ? ?, ? ?, Mavis Remphrey, Ruby Elliott, ? Rowe, Margaret Pengelly, ? ?, Pamela Kessell, Jennifer Rowe, ? ?.
Row 3: Jessie Thomas, Gillian Ede, Muriel Jenkin, Diana Armour, ? Taylor, ? James, Alison Drew, Susan Taylor, ? ?, Rosemary Olds, Tommy James, William James.
Front Row: Ian Venables, Irwin Rowe, Spencer Drew, Geoffrey Taylor, ? ?, William Pengelly.

Sancreed School about 1953-1956.
Teacher at the back - Mrs Bagley. Back Row from left: Leslie Jenkin, John Eddy, David Nicholls, Raymond Langman, Tommy James, Jessie Thomas, Brian Gendall.
Middle Row: Joyce Roberts, Sheila James, Marlene Strick, Margaret Adams, Mary Tonkin, Mary Eddy.
Front Row: Geoffrey Taylor, Alan Hosking, Michael Richards.

We used to leave home about quarter to nine in the mornings and I remember one morning coming down past the rookery which adjoined the church and the big boys were up in the trees trying to get rooks eggs. They shouted to me to go in school and come and tell them the time, but the bell rang and we were all late. Someone had told the master so we were all lined up for the cane. The ringleaders had six on their hands and smaller ones had two strokes. Someone had the cane every day.

The big ones, as we called them, would get the master

Sancreed School late 1950s.
Back Row from left: Rodney Hutchings, Richard Adams, Peter Derracot, Gilbert Pilkington, Ross Williams, Martin Jones, Geoffrey Rowe, Ivor James, Keith Jones, Billy Adams.
Second Row: Vivienne Hosking, Lesley Hawes, Margaret Roberts, Cathy Eddy, Jennifer James, Cecily Williams, Netta Gamble, Ann James, Susan Bray, June Hutchings.
Third Row: Pauline Wherry, Sandra Reynolds, Gillian Spargo, Marilyn Hosking, Rita James, Ann Kestlel, Anne Hosken, Beryl Spargo, Gina Harris, Penny Adams, Wendy Richards, Wendy Adams.
Front Row: Stephen Wherry, Nigel Gregory, Melville Wherry, Nigel George, Leonard Stevens, Terry Hawes, Bernard Thomas, Geoffrey Roberts, Derek Pilkington, Malcolm Hosking.

Sancreed School 1980.
Back Row from left: Mrs Spencer,Tracey Hosking, Joanna Kaute, Kirsty Parker, Sanchia Shaw Jane Knott, James Bryce.
Middle Row: Cynthia Wales, Josephine Matthews, Sarah Knott, Tina Adams, Jason Smith, Heath Robinson, Sabina Bray, Michael Hosking, Nigel Taylor, Amos Wales.
Front Row: Bena Smith, Philip Whitton, Sarah Tobin, Kerra Shaw, Debbie Bray, Theresa Bray, Cherry Choke, Leo Turner, Michael Whitton, Treeve Taylor.

things from the cupboard and lay them on his desk. In winter two would fetch water from the village pump, some for Mrs Martin and for the kettle for those who had lunch at school. There would be a good fire in the big and little round stoves, being lit early by the cleaner and kept well topped up by one of the bigger boys.

Country Dancing

I was about twelve when the schoolmaster retired at Christmas and he tied a bit of holly on his long cane and stuck it in the stove. Next term came two new teachers, Miss Bailey the head and a Miss Dickenson in the infants.

There was much change, first we had to line up before entering the school and there was to be no rushing out at playtimes or at any time and we should go to the offices during playtimes. We had some more interesting lessons such as crafts, question time and story time. We played games, square ball, rounders, netball, we had cricket and even played away matches, nature walks and dancing round the maypole, also we learned country dancing with Miss Bailey's sister playing the violin.

Now we the older boys, began riding our cycles to school and were allowed to put them in Mr Steven's shed at the Glebe opposite the church. In my last year, that is at thirteen to fourteen years, I sometimes drove the pony and trap to Catchall Dairy with the milk before school, getting to school about ten o'clock. I was allowed out early in the afternoons for the hay and corn harvest.

Rode bikes like lunatics!

In the spring I rode my bike both morning and after school to the Golf Links (part of our farm) to see the sheep. On one occasion after checking the sheep, I crashed into the

young schoolteacher Miss Dickenson also on bike on her way home to Penzance, we collided on the corner which had a signpost on it saying, Dangerous Corner. I picked up her bike, straightened the handlebars and sent her on her way; I said 'I rang my bell'.
She went on pushing her bike and called in the neighbour's cottage crying and they found the chain was off her bike. Someone put it on and she was able to get home. Next morning there was a lecture by the head about those who rode bikes around like lunatics" Before I left school I did many jobs on the farm. (see also Sellan)
Miss had a dog in school and little William said *"Miss, your dog did not shut his eyes in prayer time."* *"Neither did you!"* she replied.

Plan-an-gwarry   Rodney Lyon, ex Grand Bard
Grid Reference: SW 4193 2953

Location: Approximately 200 metres to the north of Sancreed Church, the site of which is now under the houses of 'Beacon Estate'.
The Tithe Map and Apportionment for the Parish of Sancreed in the Churchtown tenement names field No. 426 'Plain Gwarry'.
The current Ordnance Survey Map shows a section of the western hedge of the above field to be still curved as indicated on the Tithe Map and the author has seen this in 2007. (See Drawing).
Almost every parish had their own Plan an gwary. This was the place where wrestling matches were held and miracle plays were performed. In addition to the miracle plays the Cornish people would be entertained by occasional visits of bands of strolling players from up the country. Among other events taking place there were wrestling matches and later on miners took part in stone drilling competitions.

Although wrestling was common in England, Cornishmen were recognised as among its most skilful exponents. Henry VIII gave orders that that a number of Cornish Wrestlers should be present to compete at a great sporting event in Calais in 1521.

From early times Cornishmen enjoyed a reputation for dramatic skill. Some of these Cornish miracle plays lasted 3 days. They were most popular from 1350 to 1500, but continued much later. According to an old document, men came to watch a miracle play at Sancreed in 1780.

Plan-an-gwarry (circled).

22

SANCREED METHODIST SOCIETY IN 1767

SUNDAY, SEPTEMBER 12TH. 1762. John Wesley wrote "Between one and two I preached at Sancreed where I never was before. Abundance of strangers came from every side; and I believe not many went empty away".

John Wesley visited Sancreed again in 1768.

By 1767 there were 31 members of the Sancreed Methodist Society:-

William Edwards, tinner Tregerris; Jane Edwards; Thomas Foss, tinner; Thomas Waren, tinner; Joan Waren; John Polglase, tinner, Boswennen; William Polglase, lives with his father; Nicholas Rodda, tinner, Tranack; Philis Rodda; Jane Sowen; Honr. Rodda,Tranack Mill; Jane Rodda; John Rodda, tinner, Rosseven; Richard Rodda, tinner and William Rodda, lives with their mother; William Foss, tinner, Chehowl; John Nocholas, lives with his father; Robert Hall, Brean; Grace Skews, lives with sister; William Trembath, tinner, Tregenebras; Hom. Trembath; William Hall, labourer, Bosworthen; William Trugen, tinner; Richard Bosence, farmer, Tregenhoe; Lucretia Harry, Trevorjen; Mary Nicholls, servant; Philis Stevens, Trevean; Alex Richards, miller, Madren; Eliz. Richards; Blanch Tivey, poor; John Thomas, tinner.

Sancreed Chapel.

Sancreed Wesleyan Chapel

The Myles Chronological dates St Creet (Sancreed) Chapel as 1794. There was an interesting Wesleyan Chapel Plan dated 1817. It mentions the Chapel at Sancreet.

A new chapel was opened in 1823 and had seats for 210. In 1879 special services were held resulting in the addition to the Society of about 20 more members. The date 1886 is to be clearly seen on the outside of the top end of the former chapel; it was during this year that the chapel was renovated. The Cornish Telegraph newspaper for Thursday March 11th records the following: 'Sancreed Wesleyan Chapel. The renovation of the above chapel, which has for some time been a pressing necessity, is now under the energetic management of Mr. Quick. The front will be improved and the gallery will be removed, the loss of space to be compensated by connecting the school with the chapel. We understand that the contracts have already been agreed upon; the carpentering by Mr. Ralph H. Roberts, of St Just, and the masonry by Mr Joseph Marks, Sancreed'.

The rebuilt chapel was opened on Whitsunday 1886.

Services continued there for almost another 100 years. The last service at Sancreed Chapel (also known as Court) was on the 10th June 1984. The preacher was Rev Philip Williams and the organist was Mrs Miriam Rowe. There was a grave in the Chapel grounds in which Alexander Rowe Marrack, who died 1846, was buried.

Why was this lone grave in the chapel grounds?

To enable the sale of the chapel to take place the body of Alexander Rowe Marrack (1798 – 1846) was exhumed in August 1986 and also that of a child. There was the bottom half of a headstone on the chapel floor inscribed 1832 Tregonebris, which was probably the headstone of one of his children.

Tales fromTrevor Richards & his brother Michael

Bath Time by Trevor

"I was born on the Isles of Scilly in 1924, but came to live in Sancreed when I was a month old, my parents lived there in a little two up two down in Chapel Place.

One day when I was about three years old I decided to bath myself in mother's wooden tub in which she did the clothes washing. I clambered in with all my clothes on. Mother was not amused.

I started at Sancreed School at four years of age; Miss Bailey was the head teacher. She was very strict, and as my education continued, I was to find out."

Locked in the Church

"Putting coloured chalk in the village pump I found out was not a good idea, it resulted in me choosing one of the four canes which she kept in her desk. Two of the best on each hand, not nice. Nature lessons - After tea I decided to go up into the church tower to catch a bat to take back to school. Unbeknown to me Mr. Stevens came and locked the church door and left me stranded inside. I had to climb out on to the parapet and shout for help, Mr. Stevens let me out and I was in bother again.

My brother David was born when I was four years old. We liked springtime and when the bluebells were out we used to pick armfuls in the woods near the vicarage and take them to Mrs Lawry, (her son Harold was cobbler at Chapel Place). She used to give us a penny and we would buy a penny gob stopper from Mrs. Boon's who lived in our old house. Next day we would do the same and then David would have his gob stopper."

Aching legs one penny

"When David was born in 1929 we moved into Beacon House. It was like a mansion to us after Chapel Place. Harold Lawry with his cobblers shop had a massive machine which he used to finish off and polish the boots and shoes. It was driven by a large belt attached to a long wooden treadle. David and I used to pump this board to keep the machine going, polishing, until our legs ached. Sometimes he would give us a penny and over to Mrs. Boon's and get another gob stopper. Good old days, poor but happy.

Sancreed Beacon was our playground, also down Trerice where we climbed trees, often falling in the river! Lovely memories.

Will, my father, rang the church bells and pumped the organ. When I was about 16 years old I did likewise. Sunday evenings in the winter when Rev. Stona preached the sermon, it was like reading a book, it went on and on. Sometimes it would only be Rev. Stona, Jim Stevens and me there, sometimes one or two others. Sitting on a little stool behind the organ, I often dozed off and when Mr Stevens started playing the organ handle hit me and away pumping I would go.

The institute used to be a focal point, (I believe it still is). The billiard table was for billiards only and for the men folk, boys were not allowed near it. We used to sleep there on home guard duty and patrol up to the top of the Beacon, not nice in the middle of winter. I remember when Plymouth had the blitz, you could see on a clear night the sky was all red from the fires. When we came off patrol we would unload the 303 rounds out of the rifle. One

Sancreed Home Guard.
Standing: Jack Rowe, Bill Watters, Gordon Richards, ? ?, Charlie Olds.
Seated: Sydney Trembath, Willie Lane, George Redfern, Willie Trezise, Willie Richards.

night I remember one of the men left one round up the breech. Fortunately it went up through the roof, I expect the hole is still there! We all leapt out of our makeshift beds and thought the Germans had landed!!

When I left school at 14 I went to work market gardening with Howard Reynolds, down at Buryas Bridge. At 18 I was in the army. After training I was landed on the beaches in France. We made our way through the Low Countries into Germany."

Surprise – baby!

"I stayed in Germany until my demob, then home to the village I loved, (and still do).

At the end of 1944, when I was in Holland, I received a letter from home which said 'You will be surprised to hear that you have got a baby brother called Michael' I couldn't believe it. Eventually, I got home after the war and on my first leave I saw this blonde baby boy. After the war I bought a brand new Royal Enfield motorbike and when I came home from work Mike would be at the gate waiting. I used to pick him up and put him on the petrol tank and go from Beacon House, right around Grumbla, around Sancreed Beacon and home again.

I left Sancreed in 1952 to get married and am now living in Penzance. I still go 'home' to Sancreed and occasionally go to church, all posh now, electric power but the bells still have to be rung.

When we were young we knew everyone, but now with the council houses in the field where David and I used to play cricket it's not quite the same but at least they have water and electric! We used to carry our drinking water from the pump by the village church almost half a mile away. Rainwater was collected in a large tank by the house and was used for washing up and bathing. Candles in the bedrooms, tilley lamp downstairs, good old days."

Our father, Will Richards by Michael

"Our father, Will, was born at Tredavoe on 18 January 1898 and lived with his parents firstly at Tredavoe and then at Tolcarne Terrace, Newlyn. At age 14 he became an apprentice blacksmith at Newlyn quarry. Following a four year apprenticeship, Will followed his brothers to South Wales to work in the coal mines.

In 1916, age 18, Will joined the Welsh Regiment at Cardiff. He wanted to join his elder brother Walter, who was fighting on the Somme, however it was not to be as his service was cut short due to ill health and Pte. Richards was medically discharged in August 1917, having served for 295 days.

Will returned to Cornwall and lived with his parents at Tolcarne. On March 30 1921, he married Victoria Vida Barnes at Sennen Church. Will and Vida moved to Sancreed and lived in the top house at Chapel Place. Will was still not well and Vida and her sister started a greengrocery business with a horse and cart plying their trade between Sancreed and Sennen. Will helped out when able. Later, when his health improved, he bought a lorry and delivered fruit and vegetables all around the neighbourhood.

In 1927 Will and Vida moved to a larger house a stone's throw away at Beacon House, where they also opened up a shop selling their fruit and veg. Will lived at Beacon House for well over 40 years. They had two sons, Trevor born in 1924 with David born in 1929. Sadly Vida developed TB and died at the young age of 37.

Joyous sound of bells missed

Doris, who became his second wife, was already working in the parish as domestic servant to Miss Croager at Rosevalley. They were married by Parson John Stona at Sancreed church on 6 June 1936. The church parish notes at the time read as follows "Congratulations to the couple who fill the various posts of bell-ringers, organ blowers and cleaners of the church and day school on their marriage on 6 June. We missed the joyous sound of bells, but the ringer could not be in two places at once."

Will continued as a greengrocer and haulier for some years. He then bought a new lorry, GCV 8, a good Cornish registration number and started collecting milk from the farms in the area. His was one of a number of milk lorries that brought milk to Catchall Dairy, which was a thriving business at the time and the largest employer in Sancreed by far. I was born in 1944 at the nursing home in Penzance. In later years this traded as the Pirate Hotel until it was eventually demolished in 2002 to be replaced by luxury flats known as Penrose Court.

Beacon House was owned by a Mr Pengelly from Horsedowns, near Praze. The rent was incredibly small and never went up for many years, the landlord's part of the deal was that he would not spend any money on the property and that all improvements were to be paid for by my father, which included in later years installing water and electricity. The house had large gardens front and rear, which were always put to good use to maximise income from them. In the early years, the gardens were cultivated, where all types of vegetables and flowers were grown. Anemones and violets were very popular at the time and these were sold in the local shops in Penzance and sometimes sent 'up the line' by rail to the London markets. Taking pride of place at the end of the back garden was a pigeon loft, where Will spent many hours with his beloved birds. These would be trained, starting with a short flight 'home' from Madron Carn from where they could see Beacon House in the distance. Later they were sent by train to be released farther away. Many anxious hours would be spent with the 'pigeon clock' at the ready, to clock the birds in as they arrived back at the loft. Later both front and rear gardens were used to keep chickens. The neighbours would come and buy the excellent free-range eggs.

Wheelbarrows of water

I remember Beacon House with great fondness, however there was no running water or electricity and the weekly bath was in a tin bath in front of the 'slab', later to be replaced by a state of the art Rayburn. Rainwater was caught in a large tank at the end of the house, drained from the launders. This was fine until the dry weather came and the tank was empty. Will or Trevor or David would then put a milk churn in the wheelbarrow and push it to the village pump, (long since gone), near the church, that was the easy bit, but once filled up they had to push it up the hill. Luckily I was too young to 'enjoy' this experience, although I do remember 'priming the pump' and when the water flowed, I would fill up the churn, helping in my small way.

Eventually the council houses were built in Sancreed opposite Beacon House. On the down side, this meant that the field in which my boyhood friends David and Colin Nicholls and I endlessly played football and cricket became a housing estate; but on the positive side a trench was dug across the road to our house and we had the luxury of a cold water tap installed in the kitchen. Electricity eventually followed and this meant replacing the old wireless radio with its huge battery and an accumulator. This was a contraption made of glass, with acid and water, which needed charging up every few weeks. It was carefully placed in the car and taken to Bond Clark in Adelaide Street, where this procedure was carried out.

Trevor and David left home and married in the 1950s, then in 1962, aged 17 years, I left home to join the Royal Signals at Catterick Camp in the wilds of Yorkshire. Doris was now working at Sancreed School as a school meals supervisor, a job she loved and Will would spend his time gardening. During the summer, Doris used to take in 'lodgers' to bring in a few extra shillings Many of the lodgers came back year after year and continued to send Christmas cards right up until Doris's death in 2000.

One man band

One of Will's interests was music. He had two banjos, a piano accordion and a mandolin. The banjo was his favourite and he could play a mean tune when pushed to perform, often reluctantly. I remember a concert being held at the Sancreed Institute in the early 1950s where local people showed off their talents. Will played two or three pieces including "Bluebells of Scotland" accompanied by Tom Bottrell, from Buryas Bridge, on the bones which was greeted with huge applause. He taught Melville Rowe, brother of Cornish comedian Jethro, to play the banjo for which Melville gave him a new banjo case.

In 1971 Will and Doris were allocated a brand new 'old peoples bungalow' in Newbridge. This was a lovely home, with all mod cons and the first bathroom that they ever had! However, they always looked on Beacon House and Sancreed as their spiritual home."

Sancreed Railway!!!

Having advertised the Cornish coast and Countryside and invented the "Cornish Riviera" the Great Western Railway were keen to extend a line westward from Penzance to incorporate the then-thriving mining area of St Just, the busy the fishing port of Newlyn and the tourist potential of the Land's End and its neighbouring beaches.

Proposed to be known as the "Penzance, Newlyn & West Cornwall Railway" it would have left Penzance via a point not far from Tescos, through Bramwell Lane, to Gulval, Heamoor and Tremethick Cross. Here there was to be a junction where a line from Newlyn (for fish traffic) would have been built.

Trains would come up the Coombe to Buryas Bridge, through the valley now flooded by the reservoir and on to Sellen, Grumbla and Dowran before arriving at St Just station. An additional extension from Tremethick Cross, through Sancreed, Tregonebris and Boscawenoon would have passed just west of St Buryan Church and on to Crean to follow the valley through Tresidder Mill, past Polgigga, Skewjack and on through Trevescan to Land's End.

No Cars

This seems unbelievable today but in 1878 very few wheeled vehicles would reach the remote farms and villages. The legal "speed limit" for horse-drawn commercial vehicles was 4 miles per hour. It was to be another 30 years before the internal combustion engine would replace the horse. The first car in West Cornwall came in 1903; a steam-driven Serpolet AF2.

The route was extensively surveyed at great cost but eventually the scheme fell through.

Imagine Sancreed if the railway had been built. A holiday centre perhaps at the hub of West Penwith.

Sancreed Cricket
Record Achievement at Cricket

From The Cornishman newspaper July 15th 1936:

"The Sancreed cricket club on Thursday evening, July 9th, won the game with Keneggy and thus qualified for the final in the Runciman Cup knock-out competition. The game was played at Penzance.

Scores: Sancreed, 107 (J Osborne 39, J W Hosken and S Berryman 18 each); Keneggy, 75.

Mr J Osborne, a very prolific run-getter, of the Sancreed cricket club, has won two Woodfull's bats (one last and one this) which it is presumed constitutes a record in the West Penwith Leaguue. Hearty congratulations to Mr Osborne on his achievment."

(see also Derval)

Newbridge Cricket Team over 60 years ago.
Standing: Sam Warren, James Henry Hosking, Ronnie Oats, Thornton Jilbert, ? ?, Jim Breeyman, Douglas Laity.
Seated: Steve Berryman, Robert Lanyon, Cecil Merrifield, John Eddy, Clarence Olds, Leslie Oates.

Cricket played an important part of sporting life in Sancreed village over many decades. Above was an example of the high standard a small village achieved, 70 years ago.

CHIVERTON   Chiverton 1432 house on grassland

Chiverton. Jack & Trixie Rowe lived for a while near the dairy at Grumbla and their daughter Jennifer was born there. As small children Jennifer and Bryan, the son of Gladys & Fred Gendall, often played together. Later Jack, Trixie and Jennifer moved to Chiverton on the edge of the village. Next-door lived Jack's sister Betty and her husband Trenoweth and their daughter. Later Jennifer married and went to Canada.

Back to the Future?

David and Rachel Smart-Knight are setting a new local trend with their eco holidays. Based at Chyena, (Chiverton) and complete with compost toilets, they aim to teach a simple lifestyle change in order to help the environment.

Some of the lifestyle changes echo ways of life, long since disappeared, of our ancestors who lived in this parish previously.

NEWHAM

In the 1950s and 60s Raymond Bray occupied Newham and drove long distance lorries.

TREVORIAN   Alfred Olds 2007

"I've lived here 91 years. Trevorian Farm was bought from Mr T B Bolitho in about 1885. My paternal grandfather, James Olds, a butcher, then came here from Higher Drift. My father Alfred Olds took on the farm when he married, and I followed him.

In the other farm here was Mr Richard Pearce. When he died in 1941 his son Bert Pearce from down Trevorgans, carried on farming. When he 'packed up' I bought it from him.

I went to Sancreed School when I was five and then when I was ten I passed the Scholarship to go into the County School.

I stayed on in the County School until I was sixteen. When I was at school, I loved football but when I came home I was not allowed to play in case I got damaged for life. I had a fair, sensible upbringing really.

Farming was very bad in the '30s. My father had a struggle to keep me. My father would keep three or four sows and rear the pigs and keep so many cows. I was twenty-one when my Mother died and then Nan came here to look after us until I was married and my wife, Norah, came here and my Father lived with us.

I diversified into early potatoes and broccoli. I bought fields of broccoli off people and cut them to try to 'make a shilling'. Fortunately, early potatoes sold well and gave a good return.

My daughter Rosemary won the Open Championship for Cornwall for horse jumping when she was sixteen. She was good at Show Jumping. I picked the horses for her. There was a man called Williams up to Troon, and he had a mare called Lady of the Isle. He said to us, "Would you like to have her for a season for £50" and we said "Yes, please." Rosemary was only young and we agreed to let Lady decide for herself where to take off. Of course she sailed through. She was good.

The mad bull

We were going to Penzance about 1919 with horse and trap and when we got down to the Ropewalk, men were stopping and there was a bull. He was near the skin factory, where the Pirate pub is now, smelled the blood and that turned him wild. Men and women were climbing up the hedge and pulling up others. The bull was bellowing and people shouted to us to stop. Then the Tol Pedn bus came down. It was one of these old fashion chain drive things. The bus stopped and the bull roared and charged. All the women inside were screaming and I think the glass broke. Anyway they drove on. We returned home Heamoor way and by the time we came home, that bull had been shot and butchered.

Lucky Escape!

I was baling hay one day when, as I got off the tractor, the hem of my boiler suit got caught in the power take off shaft of the baler. I was dragged up against the toe bar of the tractor and the whizzing shaft ripped everything off me.

TREVEAN

Local golfing champion Phillip Rowe has Sancreed ancestors

William Rowe and his wife Ann were farming Trevean in the 1841 census. His fifth son Hannibal succeeded him in the 1880s at Trevean. Hannibal married Margaret Jane Pengelly and they had three children Annie, Mary and Walter.

Eventually Margaret died and in 1905 and Hannibal married a widow Mary Marks nee Grenfell. Mary was the sister of George Grenfell the famous missionary and Congo explorer. Mary and George were born at Ennis Cottage, Trannack Mill and Hannibal and Mary retired to the Mill. Walter took over Trevean in 1913 and farmed there until 1920. His son Reggie Rowe became a well respected bank manager at Helston and St Ives. Reggie's young grandson Phillip Rowe is becoming famous as a golfer.

John Williams emigrated twice!   See also Bojowans

John Williams, eldest son of Thomas Henry Williams of Bejowans, was born in 1897. The 1901 census shows him living with his grandparents Mr and Mrs Lutey at Carfury. His father, Thomas Henry Williams a widower, was flower farming at Higher Kemyell in partnership with his uncle Henry Roberts. Thomas Henry married again and had four more children then moved to Bejowans, Sancreed. John, at 17, emigrated to Australia.

John Williams: "I came to Australia in 1914 and went to work on a dairy farm, not far from Korumburra. I worked for a Scotsman from 1.30 a.m. to 7 p.m. for 10/- per week and was promised a 2/- rise after three months, if satisfactory. When I asked for this raise one morning while cutting wood, he told me I was not as good as the Australians. There was another chap, a little older than me, also working there who came from London. He could not milk. I was milking three cows to his one; three of us were milking 56 cows. So when told I was not as good as the Australians I threw the axe onto the wood heap and asked for my cheque. He was all apologies then but I said 'no' and went and packed up, got my cheque, sent a telegram to an uncle of mine in Melbourne and asked him if he knew where I could get a job on a wheat farm as I was coming on the train that day to Melbourne.

My uncle used to be a wheat buyer in Lismore, so within a week I was working on a wheat farm for 15/- a week. We put in 1,000 acres of wheat and 600 acres of oats. There were two brothers, another man and myself, three teams and I had to keep them going with seed and manure. We got the oat crop in by May 15th.

I had been writing to Kathleen Hosking for some time. We went to the same Sunday school and I took her out a few times before coming to Australia in 1914. Then my father was sick and asked me if I would like to come home and take charge of the horses and machinery. Two strings were pulling; Kathleen said, 'if you go to Australia I'm going too'. Well I thought it out and decided I did not know much about machinery and it was a good chance to learn and I did learn quite a lot that came in useful in later years. Then Kathleen and I had the chance to have Trevean Farm, Sancreed, so we married".

Five years later in 1925 they decided to go to Australia.

After selling up, while John and Kathleen were waiting for their ticket, they stayed with her sister, Elsie, and her husband, James Henry Care, then living at Trevider, St Buryan. Later they were to meet his uncle, William Henry Care, in Australia.

John and Kathleen and four small children, Kathleen, Sidney, Henry, and Clifford, left England on board the steam ship "Demosthenes" on 9th October to settle in Australia. On 15th November 1925 Kenneth was born at sea in Australian waters off Western Australia. During the next few years seven more children were born, making 6 boys and 6 girls; the last two were twins.

Norman and Revena Pengelly

When Norman Pengelly came back from the 1914-18 War he farmed 50 acres of Bosliven St Buryan. In 1925 he moved into Trevean, Sancreed.

Once while he was milking the cows, lightning went straight in through the doorway and struck the third cow down, and the second one was singed. The one he was milking was not touched. It went out through the opening and caught fire to the hayrick. The fire brigade was called but they couldn't do much with it. They pulled the rick all abroad but the cows would not eat the hay after.

Norman, Revena, and four children Geoffrey, John, Reggie, and Revena moved to Budock in 1938.

Trevean Farm.

William John Thomas

"My Grandfather who was farming at Halwyn in Paul parish had a letter from the Bolitho estates offering him Trevean Farm, which he took over on Michaelmas day 1939.

He died early in 1945 and my father Richard Benjamin Thomas married Betty Nicholls of Trevedran, St Buryan and moved from Halwyn that year to Trevean. It was here my sister Elizabeth and I were brought up.

In 1945 my father Ben Thomas with my Uncle Cyril Eddy and Mr A J Olds and others started the first Western Area ploughing match. It was held on the day I was born. There was only one cup, and that was for the best ploughman in Sancreed Parish, this my father won.

In 1964 he became Chairman of the N F U of Cornwall, and Chairman of West Penwith District Council 1970 - 1972. In 1968 I married Diane Wallis of Helston and she came to live at Trevean. My parents went to live at Rissick, St Buryan. We brought up our 3 children John, Stuart and Cheryl there. I was on the Sancreed Parish council and also Penwith District Council and have been Churchwarden of Sancreed Parish Church for nearly 30 years. My wife, Diane, has played the Church organ since 1980.

Diane: "Mrs Booton, the organist, left the Church and I was the only one that could play at all so I volunteered. In 1980 I believe that was and I'm still there! Mrs Booton's husband was a local preacher. Lovely people, they used to live in the School House there. Anita George was the previous organist before and Vivienne Hosking also. Mrs Booton was determined to go and live in Shropshire, but her husband didn't want to go. They were going on the Friday and the Vicar asked had I been given the keys. I wasn't given the keys until Mrs Booton was in the furniture van ready to move off!

When they got there Mr Booton was ringing up because he wanted to come back but his wife wouldn't hear of it and he died shortly afterwards. It's very hard to move at that age and they had many friends here. They were both in their 80's."

Sancreed Feast

Diane: "Whit Sunday is Sancreed Church Feast and we usually have a special service in Church and we have a lovely roast dinner in the Williams Hall. All the ladies come and bring their roast beef and vegetables and Yorkshire puddings and all sorts of sweets.

Everyone comes along and joins in and have a really good hour or two for lunch. For Feast the Church is always decorated in red and white flowers. Even the altar cloths are red. It's the fire, Whit Sunday, the Pentecost."

Diane and William John at a recent Harvest Lunch.

Silver Jubilee Community Spirit

William John: "For the Queen's Silver Jubilee we had a big event up in the fields and the Parish Council asked Diane to organise it and get some helpers."

Diane: "Yes, it was a Sports Day for the children. We organised a sports afternoon, tea, with cakes and buns and all sorts. The bunting was up. I only had to ask for help and people responded by supplying everything required.

Our son Stuart married Tamsin Hocking of Trengothal St Levan in 1994 and now lives in Trevean with their 2 children Benjamin and Katie. Stuart has recently joined the Parish council and is the 4th generation of the Thomas family to farm Trevean.

In 1999 Mr Alverne Bolitho asked us to take on Trewidden Farm and my eldest son John now lives and farms there".

CHAPTER 2

DRIFT / CATCHALL AREA

DRIFT RESERVOIR & DAM

Time was

In this valley bordered by Drift, Trevean, Treganoe, Sellan, Skimmel Bridge and Trewidden, beside a little stream was the home of the rabbit and fox. Daffodils and early potatoes were grown. Local people rambled there picking blackberries, or visiting their friends at Sellan. Children set up rival camps.

John Richards Jnr: "We must have been about 12 to 15 kids altogether who played in the valley from Nathcothan to Sellan particularly on Saturdays. We all had camps in different places. We were in different rival gangs. We used to say that our children were the last generation to do that." A place of peace and tranquillity.

The Scheme

In 1951 a joint water scheme to serve the whole of the Land's End Peninsula was resolved by Penzance and St Ives Borough Councils.

The reservoir would have a capacity of between 290 and 300 million gallons with a daily output of around 30 million.

Work on the Dam was started by Messrs Robert McAlpine & Sons on 1st March 1959 and was completed on 1st April 1961. Alterations to the original design of the Dam under part of the Spillway was necessitated as during excavations for foundations it was found that a small area of decomposed granite would only carry 2 1/2 tons per square foot instead of 4 1/2 tons per square foot for which the Dam was designed.

Pure water from the Drift works is circulated to the rest of Penwith via a complex pumping network and several smaller reservoirs.

One at Chywoone serves Newlyn, Mousehole and some areas east of the town. Another at Cryor supplies St.Just, Pendeen and areas along the north coast whilst another at Leah takes care of the demands of the Lands End area, Sennen, St Buryan and St Levan.

Occupiers around the valley accepted the inevitable, that their land would be flooded when the dam was built.

Only one now remained - Mr Reynolds, whose farm, Nanquitho, was to be flooded, held out because he said he would be left with a useless piece of land. Later, he withdrew his opposition to save taxpayers money.

Clearing the site

For a year or two before the dam was built Terry Shorland and a team from the Bolitho Estate were employed felling the larger trees, which were upstream from the proposed dam. This was in the summer. In the winter he carried on game keeping. In 1971 he joined the Water Board.

Tommy James: (see Little Sellan) "I remember when the work on the dam started. Billie Berryman from Newbridge , our former employee went there to work. He worked with Stanley Thomas who had a contract to clear the valley. He, with several others, was cutting down trees and burning them. Chain saws were going every day. They had a contract to clear the valley before the start of building the dam. These men were then employed by Sir Alfred MacAlpine on the dam.

It was an eye opener for us as youngsters to see such a big project. I can remember when we were home on holidays hearing the hooter going at 12.30 down at the dam, and that was to tell the workmen it was lunchtime. The canteen was up in the hill and if you were down in the pit you had to climb up three or four ladders to get your dinner and at 1pm the hooter went and you had to go down the ladder again.

The work was done by mainly imported labour, including many Irish workmen. You could see the dam rising daily. There was a concern at the time because after they had plugged the wall it had filled up so quickly."

William John Thomas: "When they sealed off the dam Margaret Jeffery, my cousin down Kerris Vean myself, and Robert Eddy of Trenuggo used to ride ponies down there for weeks galloping around in the water as it was filling up."

The dam was built none too soon for in the dry summer of 1959 West Cornwall had been experiencing drought conditions and water shortage.

The dam was opened by the Housing Minister, Henry Brooke, on 16 June 1961.

Having an abundant supply of fresh water was a wonderful achievement for the health and well-being of the people of West Cornwall.

Most of Nanquitho Farm is now in the reservoir. The house there was also knocked down; perhaps the only one in the valley.

It must have been sad for the occupiers to see their land disappearing under the water.

Fishing

Terry Shorland's home lies at the edge of the lake looking over the reservoir, the birds, the fishing and he helped with the stocking. "8000 rainbow trout were put in the reservoir in 1962. They came from the famous Loch Leven trout fisheries through Mrs Williams. She had 33,000 acres of land in Scotland. There was no life in the reservoir so we got many buckets of shrimps from Stithians reservoir. We had wire netting put around them to prevent them being eaten. There are a tremendous number of shrimps now". There are other fish as well including brown trout. The reservoir is an ideal place for anglers.

Birdwatching

The place is a haven for birds and birdwatchers. Many varieties of birds are to be found there. Some of them are quite rare. For much of the year it is the home of over 80 swans, and an equal number of Canadian geese. Upstream there is a hide.

The Dam, today.

The reservoir and dam add greatly to the charm of the area for locals and visitors alike. Terry has been collecting bin bags filled with the out-of-date products from the bakery and supplying the birds with their main source of food.

At the request of Bolitho Estates, which manages the lake and owns the fishing rights, the bakery has stopped Mr Shorland's supply, leaving the birds to fend for themselves.

The situation, according to the RSPCA, is especially grave at the present time because birds are unable to fly because their feathers are moulting.

Edward Bolitho, manager of the estate, said it was decided to control the number of swans, which had increased to as many as 100, for their own safety.

"It was creating problems not only for the fishing but for the swans themselves," he said.

"The birds are in danger of being caught in the fishing lines. It's all being done to keep a sense of balance on the reservoir."

Since the bakery supply has ended Terry Shorland has been buying bread for the swans and feeding them with grass cuttings supplied by neighbours, "I'm heartbroken. They're like part of my family." said Mr Shorland. "I've been feeding these birds a long time. I've got them so tame they eat the buttons of my shirt.

A mallard duck used to come in the house sometimes. I would open my door in the morning and she'd be quacking for eats. Eventually a fox got her.

A swan with a broken wing has been here seven years."

Drift Reservoir is a beauty spot; well worth a visit. Walk on the dam. Study the birds or sit in your car and enjoy the view.

Latin cross and tin streaming

Above the old leat, in a wooded area about 120 yards downstream of the Drift dam, is a granite slab on which there is a Latin cross in relief on both sides. It was discovered c1850 when a field at Higher Drift Farm was cleared of stones.

Long ago, legend has it, pilgrims from Jerusalem came to Madron Church. They would visit the cross and go on to Drift Mill for bread flour, then to Chyanhall and finally Lamorna or Mousehole.

A river divides Sancreed and Madron parishes and below Drift dam there is a very scenic meeting place of the 3 parishes of Paul, Sancreed, and Madron.

Many centuries ago much tin was 'streamed' in the river here and in the 'bottoms' between Drift Mill and Nancothan Mine were two fields known as Parc Enys and The Glance, of which it was traditionally said: *"Parc Enys and The Glance*
Are worth more than Newlyn Mousehole and Penzance"
so rich was the alluvial tin that lay beneath them.

The two fields mentioned are on the Madron side of the river but the rich alluvial tin, 'deep as a house' it has been said, traversed the river and was equally abundant on the Sancreed/Paul side.

Tin streaming was practised from earliest times long before much mining commenced. Avarack and Nancothan mines were still working in 1858 and known also as Drift Moor Consols, at Lower Drift. The Drift River makes a sharp curve to the south at Lower Drift and the mine workings were partly in the bend of the river but mainly between it and the Lower Drift-Penzance road. There were six lodes.

A short way down stream at 12ft beneath the then surface, a curious pumping engine was discovered dating from when the stream was last worked. It consisted of a wooden beam 14 ft long, pivoted on a tripod. At one end was attached a very large stone, and a pump rod; on the other a square box with a bottom that opened. When this box was filled with water its weight overbalanced the pump and stone at the other end of the beam, discharging the water and reaching its former position and this ingenious device was often used to pump out small shallow mines.

Drift village.

Arthur Cecil Todd in his book The Cornish Miner writes of Lark in Utah, "Lark is the Little Cornwall of the desert. Even boasting a pub appropriately called the Drift Inn."

DRIFF MILL - Desirable Freehold Estate, Grist Mill, For Sale.

This advertisement appeared in the West Briton, March 21st 1823

"To be sold by auction on Monday the 31st of March 1823 by Three o'clock in the afternoon, at Pearces Hotel in the Town of Penzance, the fee simple and inheritance of all that well accustomed Grist Mill and tenement, containing about seven acres of tillable land called LOWER DRIFF MILL Situate in the parish of Sancreed, now in the occupation of John Bure.

The MILL has a constant supply of water and is well situated, offering every facility for carrying on business on an extensive scale. For a view apply to the occupier of the premises, and for financial particulars to Nicholas Tremewen at Bosfranken, in St Buryan or to

Messrs Wallis & Roberts, Attornies, Helston."

Taken from **Hicks** *Family* by Rie M. Fletcher & Joan R Fortes

"Thomas Hicks was the miller of Drift Mill from about 1844 until he emigrated to Auckland, NZ in 1859.

In 1842, at Madron, he married Elizabeth, daughter of John & Mary (nee Giles) Williams of Gulval.

Thomas was the Sunday school superintendent at Drift Sunday School and a lay-preacher.

Thomas Hicks's barley flour was in demand because it was much cheaper than wheat flour and this is borne out in the Drift Mill account of Richard Grenfiel. Loaves of bread were made from the barley flour, as well as the acclaimed Cornish pasty. Traditionally, the 'proper' Cornish pasty was filled with potatoes, turnip and a little meat, for the pasty was a meal in itself. It was the 'takeaway' of the time, for the miners and field workers could take this convenient tasty food for consumption at 'croust' time.

A prized possession of his descendants is Thomas Hicks's little mill ledger bound in faded black leather with a hinged brass clasp. After the index, the first entry is dated July 1855 and is for James Tippet to Thomas Hicks. Perhaps James Tippet was a baker, for in the week 23-30 July, he purchased 3 of best flour @ 56/- sack, 4 bushels of flour @ 27/- each, a bushel of grain 5/-, a hundredweight of bran @ 6/- and a sack of flour not charged for. James Tippet's account on page 127 is the last recorded for sales in the ledger and is for July 1859, the amount of twenty two pounds six shillings and four pence halfpenny, being marked "settled".

There were great attractions for the Hicks family to emigrate. Thomas may have believed his troublesome 'miller's cough', caused by the long years of dusty grinding at the Drift Mill, would improve in a climate that was free of snow and cold in the winter. He may have thought the lives of his children would be better in a new land.

The Auckland Provincial Government needed men who were artisans and tradesmen and those who had a proven agricultural background. (There was farm land with Drift mill).

Thomas paid the ninety four pounds fare for his family and having a good reference he was well equipped to receive free land. Another son Robert Matthew was born in March

1859 and on the 10th October that year they embarked at Plymouth for New Zealand on the ship "African" of 888 tons register. The Hicks in the second cabin were more fortunate than those of the steerage passengers as their victualling allowances seemed so much more generous.

Because three of the children were between the ages of five years and eighteen years, there would be sixty acres to add to the eighty acres for Thomas and Elizabeth - 140 acres of good fertile well-watered farmland, handy to the town sounded excellent. Opportunity beckoned.

Thomas and Elizabeth Hicks arrived at Auckland, New Zealand on 30 January 1860, after 17 weeks at sea. Neither Thomas, his wife or their four children would ever see their native Cornwall again.

Of their family—Thomas Jnr had 12 children, Elizabeth 8, Christianna 8 and Robert none.

Many years later

Percy, Christianna's son, told his family that whilst on leave in the First World War, he had gone to visit a relative living near Drift. He said that it was dark by the time they had finished dinner, and in the rather gloomy light they had walked a distance and then down a lane, the sounds of their footsteps striking stones on the path. The mill building loomed up in front of them, dreary, cold and damp and all around them was the sound of a heavy rushing and thudding of water as the waterwheel turned constantly. Perhaps if he had seen the mill in the pleasant light of the Cornish summer he might have been more enthusiastic about it, but that is the memory he passed on - a stone building - cold and damp, and sixty years later he could still recall the foreboding sense of fear that enveloped him that night. *From Hicks' Family book*

The Richards family of Drift Mill

Richard Sampson Richards, born at Ludgvan, was a miller at Chinoy/Treen Mill and later at Rissick, St.Buryan. In 1859 he was miller at Drift followed by his son Richard Sampson Richards Junior who bought all the property in 1894.

In 1859 Richard Sampson Richards Jnr. had been one of seven Trustees who had land assigned to them to build a Bible Christian Chapel at St Buryan. It was completed in 1860.

Richard Richards, Ludgvan + Elizabeth.

1812-1871 Richard Samson Richards + Grace Johns at St Buryan.

1841-1912 Richard Samson Richards Jnr miller Drift + 1868 Priscilla Boase, St Buryan,

1879-1920 Richard John Boase Richards miller of Drift + Ethel Bailey (Daisy).

Their children were John, Theodore, Monica, and Sydney.

Monica James, Drift recalls

"There is a painting by Elizabeth Forbes (1897) of my father, by the 'new' mill, dreaming of a princess. That was the mill that milled our corn. You could turn the water to work the old mill wheel on the other side of the mill house, which had been done until uncle came down and told us that old mill was dangerous. (In 1817 land at Drift was leased to John Stevens to build the 'new' mill within 6 months!)

In this valley too there was a water wheel for the hat and the blanket factory.

I can remember the blanket factory, which had a large rack. Teasels were grown round about here in what was called the 'Rack Field' and used in the rack to tease out the wool. I do not remember the blanket factory working, but when I was young I spoke to an older person who did. The Rack Field was named in the 1840 tithe map. (The blanket factory seems to have been in use from well before 1800 until after 1850).

Drift Mills House, where I live, was originally a thatched farmhouse. There was a chapel out at the back. My brother John Richards used it for stores and now it has become a house. The chapel was in use until 1861 when the new one was built.

'Dream Princess'

The Richards, Norths and the Reynolds were founder members of that Drift chapel. On its 100th anniversary descendants of founder members were invited to be present.

At Govail were two blacksmiths, Clemens and James and there were two carpenter's shops in Drift. One used by Ruskin Hosken whilst his cousin worked in the other, across the way.

Wendy Richards downstream of the dam at 3 parish boundaries - Madron, Paul and Sancreed.

I've heard mother say that the people from Trewidden would send over corn for milling. Father would mill the corn whilst the horses were being shod. The horseman would pick up the bread flour place it on the horses' back and return at once to Trewidden. They took a short cut across the river. The bread flour being still warm the housekeeper would make bread with it that day.

We don't like eggs

Our neighbour Billie, always said he didn't like eggs. My mother said to him, "It's a funny thing to me Billie - how are there so many eggshells on your ash pile?" "No, no, we don't like eggs". Billie was coming up the road with father one day. They were chatting away and laughing. My Father put his hand on top of Billie's head and squashed it all down and all these eggs ran down his face. Father said to him "You are a dirty old rogue Billie you'll die in your shoes", and do you know he did die in his shoes. He was down the valley here picking daffodils in the meadow when he died. He rolled down to the bottom of the hill and there he was found with daffodils in his hand.

One day we were down in the mill yard with father. He had a little Fiat. He would strip it down. John, my eldest brother, was helping. The three of them had oilcans but I didn't. I was pulling at my father's arm to say, "Isn't there one for me?" He went off and found me a little oilcan to oil this little Fiat.

Father always wore a buttonhole and he had a twinkle in his eye. I cried bitterly when he died. I was three and Sidney one and a bit. Theo was six and John was seven.

Millstone headstone

My father died of typhoid in 1920. We had police here front and back and all the drains were dug up. If mother needed to buy anything she had to put a note in a basket and give it to the policeman. All the linoleum was taken up and burnt and mother afterwards creosoted the floors. We could never find out how father got typhoid. A millstone was hanging on the wall in the mill and mother decided she would like to have it for a headstone for my father.

Dick Bottrell had worked for my grandfather and stayed here and worked until he was too old.

Mother was so artistic. Her drawings were beautiful. She also did a lot of copper work. She went to Falmouth Art School to learn drawing and then Camborne School of Mines to learn to do the copper work. She used to travel around quite a bit but when father died she had to stay at home to mind the business. She was 38 years old.

Mother was busy. She ran the mill and could turn her hand to anything. She was only 38. She milked the cows – although at first she was so frightened.

When mother had to mill and I was crying John would cuddle me and put me back to bed. Mother had a light on the landing. She could see the light and know we were all right. She had to mill at night because she had to look after us by day.

Most of the farmers around here, who were entitled to have water from the river, would have a water butt on wheels pulled by a pony. As children we would dam up the water in summer and they would come down with buckets and fill up their barrels. It was a bit of fun! I was one girl with three boys. I was dressed as a boy, hair cut like a boy.

Theo and John were very clever at making things. We made bows and arrows. We had geese, so plenty of tail feathers. Theo made us whistles with sycamore wood. Down in the yard while Mother was milling I fell in the leat. Theo got me out and brought me in the mill and sat me on a sack of corn and called mother. By the time she got me in I was shaking. I had to stay in bed a long time. Mother had a home help and people in the village were very kind. I did not go to school until I was eight.

Theo used to run into Lescudjack School with his hoop after taking the milk down to Catchall Factory. I milked and made butter and attended to the poultry. We had 17 acres and I kept pedigree goats during the war.

Praying Betsy

All down through the valley were apple trees. Every sort of apple tree you could think of. We had this sow called Betsy. Betsy was certainly a *pig!!* She ate so many apples that when she struggled up into the mill yard she was blown up like a barrel They all came down from the village to see Betsy all blown up. If you had any thing wrong with animals you would send for Dick Jenkin. Mother got Dick Jenkin a thick knitting needle. He sharpened it and stuck it right in Betsy's stomach. All this fermented gas came out. That saved her life.

Another day we had a terrible flood. The whole of the valley was full of water. With the force of the water you could hear the great boulders being rolled along. A piece of the meadow was washed away. Father had had a big garage built down there and mother had it made into pigs' houses. We went down to have a look and there she, Betsy, was feet up on the door and her nose resting on her feet. Otherwise she would have drowned. These pigsties were full of water. We called her *Praying Betsy* after that.

On leaving school my brother John went to work in Taylor's Garage at Penzance to learn engineering. Theo was a carpenter working with James' in Penzance. Sydney became a carpenter with Peaks in Newlyn.

Boyhood of John Richards Junior

John " There must have been about 12 to 15 kids altogether who played in the valley from Nancothan to Sellan particularly on Saturdays. We all had camps in different places and we were in different rival gangs. We used to say that our children were the last generation to do that. Our son Paul used to fish in the dam and later his brothers learned to fish there too."

Richards Brothers of Drift

Monica's brother, John Richards, started his own engineering business in 1934, servicing cars and diesel engines. Sometimes mining people came and asked for advice. On one occasion he was asked how to get an engine out of a round house that had been built around it. Later, Theo and Sydney also became involved in the family business. When the war started Theodore was driving tractors on the farms for the war effort and Sydney was in the army.

Land was compulsorily purchased from the Richards family in 1938 for the building of Drift Dam.

John was an expert on diesel injectors and cleaning them. He used to clean the injectors for the diesel trains when they first came to Penzance.

John Theo and Sydney Richards set a cannon in place at Penzance Library. It has since been stolen!

Churchill

John Richards Jnr: The Richards brothers made and adapted a machine they called *"Churchill"*. It was a U.S. White half track troop carrier which they converted into a big four wheeled vehicle with a massive engine and on the back was a rig and pulleys to lift what was required.

This equipment was used to good effect in a hair-raising incident when a large Fiat bulldozer, owned by Jack Eddy of Lower Leah and driven by John Tonkin, got stuck in the mud at Penzance harbour. In a race against the rising tide and in front of hundreds of onlookers, the Churchill managed to winch the bulldozer clear and under Ross Bridge just in time. John Richards, operating the Churchill was told by his uncle, "You stay in the cab and if you feel the wire rope breaking you get down underneath right away because if it breaks and goes back over the cab, there's no knowing what will happen", such was the strain on the winch!

The Richard's brothers went on to build a crane for MacSalvers at the workshops and to do much repair work for companies like Penlee Quarries and Holmans Dry Dock.

The Churchill was much used to help Freeman Sanders at Trembath Mills lift and move on and off the test bed, engines he was experimenting on".

Arthur Freeman Sanders

The success of Arthur Freeman Sanders in his experiments which developed the modern diesel car, tractor, and fishing boat, has never been fully publicised.

Freeman Sanders's speciality was combustion chamber design. This ensured complete and instantaneous combustion and lack of 'diesel knock'.

A heat exchanger meant that the air so heated, when fed into the engine, contributed significantly to the smooth running of it and economy of fuel.

Freeman Sanders designs were far ahead of their time.

First London diesel taxi adapted at Trembath Pottery.

R101 airship

After serving in the First World War, Freeman Sanders had joined Listers of Dursley to work on petrol and diesel engine development. He designed a very successful range of diesel engines for Lister. He also designed a prototype 6 cylinder aluminium diesel engine for the R101 airship This most unfortunately blew up during trials when an over zealous mechanic filled it with lubricating oil. He later joined Fowlers of Leeds, guiding the company's change-over from steam to diesel engines.

In 1940 he founded the Freeman Sanders Engine Company. With a small force, including one or two famous names, they were consulting and development engineers in the field of high speed diesel engines. In 1946 the company moved to Trembath Mills, near Newlyn.

The diesel engine for the successful Standard Ferguson tractor was designed and developed. It was also installed in an early model of the Standard Vanguard car. **The first London taxis to be diesel powered used this engine also. They were the first**

to be approved by the Metropolitan Police on noise grounds. Amongst other clients of the firm were Rolls Royce, David Brown, Fords (a tractor engine), and Marshalls of Gainsborough (also a tractor engine).

Freeman Sanders and John Richards of Drift

John Richards Jnr. "Freeman Sanders developed the engine and then my father would be using materials to make the pistons. He would run them on the engine dynamometers for so many hours to destruction or whatever, and then take them all to pieces to have them analysed. There was a lot of very technical work going on there at Trembath Mill. Back in the 40s and early 50s Dad (John Richards Snr.) had a machine shop at the garage with lathes, milling machines, planers, threading machines and all sorts. He

used to do machining for Sanders. That was the connection prior to Dad giving up the machine shop. He put all the diesel equipment in the machine shop in 1955/56. Sanders then used to send up all the fuel pumps up to be built with his own parts that he had made."

Barbara Lever was secretary to Freeman Sanders 1949/51. She remembers that Mr John Richards came regularly down to the laboratories and Mr Sanders dealt quite a lot with him.

Dad (John Richards), sons Andrew, David, Paul and mum Anne.

The Richards Engineering Business was moved from Drift in 1989, to Cardrew Industrial Estate Redruth. Managed by John Richards Jnr. and sons it is still going strong after 70 years.

Miss Katherine North – a resident at Drift

"Mr Martin was the Headmaster at Sancreed School. I don't remember him taking lessons at all. "Take out your geography books, take out this and that and get on with it!" Miss Williams from Pendeen was the other teacher. My mother was a Reynolds, one of ten children from Paul. She had been a teacher. I learned most from her. I could read before I went to school. I had an operation for appendicitis when I was seven and was away for some while. Mother tutored us for our scholarship which we had to pass to go to the County School. Cora James the Drift blacksmith's daughter and I passed and we went into County School at 10 years old. We were great friends. She died at 17. Her father's blacksmiths shop was by Drift Chapel. We often heard the ring of the hammer on the anvil. Also at the crossroads were two carpenters shops.

I remember Jack Hosken the carpenter was the first one around to have a wireless. It was not called a radio then. We were invited to come to his bungalow and have a listen with headphones on. You couldn't hear very much. It must have been in the early/mid 1920s.

I remember the first wireless we had. To change the station you had to open it and put your hand inside somewhere. We used to take accumulaters down to the garage to have them recharged. It was quite a performance. I remember my brother Clifford and I would go on Sunday to Sunday School and Chapel but in the evening in winter we would be left at home. While our parents were out we would put on Radio Luxemberg. They

Miss North, 50 years organist at Drift Chapel.

were nice programmes. The BBC also had good programmes in the afternoons, they usually had orchestras from different locations.

I remember when the dam was declared open and sitting on the grass watching the ceremony going on below. It was a lovely fine day. Our fields were taken and incorporated in the dam. As children we used to walk out there, through our moor and then through Mr Nicholls' moor and out to the woods to play.

After County School I taught for two terms at St Buryan School where Miss Beaulah Wright of Newlyn was a teacher. At college her sister Sylvia became my closest friend and we remained friends all her life.

When I left Southlands I taught first at St Teath. I was there when the evacuees came. In 1941 I was appointed to Fourlanes School and was there for 20 years. I lodged most of that time with James Henry and Elsie Care who had come there from St Buryan. I still keep in touch with the family at Christmas.

I followed mother's sister Marian Reynolds as organist at Drift chapel. She died in 1950 and the job was passed on to me and I am still at it! I've got the hymn tunes for Sunday here. My sight is not 100 per cent. John Magor makes enlarged copies of the hymns for me. (She was given a certificate for 50 years as organist in 2000!)

Lockerbie

In December 1988 my brother Clifford's granddaughter Sophie North was killed in an explosion on a US plane which crashed at Lockerbie in Scotland killing 270 persons. She was an only child and her father, Michael North, had lost his wife not long before with breast cancer."

Drift Chapel

The old Bible Christian Chapel was situated behind Drift Mills House in the lane that led to the watermill. In 1858 Mr Hicks, who had recently joined the Society, lent his barn for a missionary meeting because *"our chapel is very small!"*

The old chapel became a store and is now a private house.

Land was leased for a new chapel at Drift crossroads for a term of 99 years from 24 June

1861. The lease was between William Rawlings of the first part and James Gilbert, John Nicholas, Russell Charles Clemence, Charles Clemence the younger, Richard Sampson Richards, Joseph Sampson Richards, Pascoe Richards, John Charles Penrose Osborne, Benjamin Hocking, and William Dunn. When Miss Diamond from Breage preached even this chapel was so crowded that some could not gain admission.

In 1961, Drift Chapel was given to its Trustees in a deed of gift by Mrs Mary Francis Williams of Trewidden.

Lloyd Reynolds "My grandfather farmed Bellogus in Paul from about 1870 and the family attended Drift chapel.

Going back a bit, the Methodists were very religious. My uncle said they weren't even allowed to shave on a Sunday. Father went to Drift chapel. On Sunday mornings they would go to prayer meeting at 10am before Sunday school at 11 am. At 2 pm Chapel service, and 6 pm they had the evening service. Then occasionally on Monday evening they would have another service.

Drift residents used to take their buckets down to the pump in Pump Lane about 100 yards down on the road from Drift to Chyanhall to obtain their drinking water; but never on a Sunday!

There used to be a wind band at Drift in the *Town Hall*. The Town Hall was the room upstairs in the carpenter's shop where they played billiards"!

Spurgeon Cottage built 1882

Spurgeon Cottage in the village of Drift was named after Dr Charles Spurgeon (1834-1892). People living at Drift at the time believed that it was built for his wife. He was an English Baptist preacher, author, and editor and also Pastor of the Metropolitan Tabernacle from 1861 until his death. He had ministered to a congregation of almost 6000 people there each Sunday. He founded a pastors' college (1856), an orphanage (1867). He died in 1892 and was considered one of the greatest preachers of the 19th century.

Small world!

In 1922 a young man Rev Bertram Woods was training at Cliff College for the Methodist Ministry. On Sundays he attended Levenshulme Wesley Chapel, Manchester. There he met a young lady, whom he eventually married. She was a niece of the evangelist Rev Luke Wiseman. She was also mother's best friend.

About fifty years later he came to Cornwall to Drift. As a sick visitor he called on my own mother who was delighted to see him. She still had the wedding present she had received from her friend, his late wife, 50 years before.

Clemens, the Blacksmiths

Charles Clemens was a blacksmith at Drift and also the school inspector. His brother William born 1849 became a blacksmith in St Buryan. William's son William immigrated to Australia in 1912 where one day a 28-foot snake came down the chimney!

In 1914 William's daughter Maud, a teacher at St Buryan School, was about to get married, and the children collected for a wedding present. She caught typhoid along with 50 others in the village from an infected well. She was one of the 6 who died. The children bought a wreath with the wedding present money.

HIGHER DRIFT   Sheep in Market Jew Street

Betty Olds 2001: "Tom Mike Olds, my father, was a butcher as well as a farmer. He would go to Helston Market on Mondays for cattle and Truro on Wednesdays where he bought his sheep for slaughtering. These were brought down to Penzance by train. Then somebody would meet the train and drive them nearly three miles out here to Higher Drift. (Imagine driving sheep up Market Jew Street in Penzance!) If he had much meat left over he would get a wagonload of ¼ cwt blocks of ice from Newlyn and keep it in an icehouse until needed.

Father had a lot of business. I think everybody in Treen and Penberth had meat from us. He supplied Lands End Hotel. He used a horse and cart at first, later he had a car. He thought electricity was wonderful but he wouldn't have a telephone. He said they'd be ringing all hours of the night, Lands End Hotel and everybody else. Sometimes visitors would come out to the hotel not having booked. The hotel would send a wire into town and a girl would come out with a telegram.

Father used to race pigeons, which were sent by train as far as the Midlands. It is wonderful the way they can find their way home.

Hector, one of our horses, was taken to go to war (WW1). We were very upset. We were sure he would be shot. Our horses were Hector, Madam and the cob Tom. I used to ride Old Tom sidesaddle up to Trevorian. Cousin Alfred Olds was an only child. From there I'd come back down Drift and up the road. I had a lovely childhood. I was the only girl. I had two brothers, Aubrey and Cyril.

I had pet rabbits which increased in numbers to around 30. Father said this was too many so he sold some of them on the butcher's round!

We had a lovely Christmas party at the Vicarage. Then the next night Mrs Martin of the Schoolhouse would invite us up. We couldn't have the fun like we did at the vicarage but we had a lovely meal. Poor father had to drive to Sancreed two nights following with a pony and cart to bring us home.

After Sancreed I used to go to Penzance to school on the back of my brother Cyril's bike. Then he had appendicitis and died. Father bought a car after he had a nasty accident riding Cyril's bike at Trereife Lodge.

We had an orchard where we grew fruit; gooseberries, raspberries, and blackcurrants. We had a 60 ft greenhouse, grapes in the top and tomatoes in the bottom. Mother looked after our garden and grew a lovely lot of flowers.

I'll shoot you if you steal my corn

The dogs on the farm became very noisy at night, so father stayed up one night and hid away. He found some people coming up from Catchall, climbing up through the trap hatch into the barn and pouring corn down through into an open sack. He caught them. He had his gun in his hand. He told them if he found them there again he would shoot them. He wouldn't hesitate. They were stealing our corn.

I learned to play the violin. I was so nervous when I went in for exams although I did pass them. I played a lot in London. I led the orchestra when I was at college.

Debutante presented at Court wearing the gown I had made

"I learned dressmaking and in the third term I made a court gown. Everything had to be sewn by hand. Miss Davis, the art teacher, took me down the Mall to see a girl sitting in her great car with her mother and father, waiting to be presented in Buckingham Palace, wearing the court gown I had made in my third term at college. I was very proud of that dress".

HIGHER DRIFT   Hilda Nicholls

"When we were first married, Percy and I were up in our home farm for six years. We sold most of the milk at the door. People came up from the village with their jugs. What was left over was sent to Catchall Dairy. Tom Mike Olds, our neighbour, in his later years had been attacked by someone with an iron bar. He spent a long time in hospital and was lucky to be alive. When he died in 1951 we worked the two farms and let the home farm house to a workman. Percy said to me "Do you want a washing machine?" I said, "No, I want a milking machine first!"

Desmond Nicholls

"In the early sixties Peter Scott, who formed the Wild Fowl Trust at Slimbridge, landed in our top field at Higher Drift because he couldn't make the Lands End airport with a glider.
On our 25th wedding anniversary I had a flying lesson. Janet went with me. She sat in the back doing photography. The pilot took us out over St Michaels Mount and said "Now Nicholls you take over". I flew from Drift Dam to St Just Airport. I said "For heavens sake take over the controls to land because I'm not going to land it!"

CATCHALL

Catch All Inn

For a short period around 1850, Gabriel Hosken, a tin streamer, was a publican at Lower Hendra Cottages, where he and his wife Elizabeth lived for a while. This appears to have been a beer house, which apparently acquired the nickname of Catch All.
"We pass the quaintly named Catch'all Inn at Lower Hendra," is a quote from Murray's *Handbook of Cornwall* published in 1893.
Beer houses – (kiddlywinks or winks as they were known in Cornwall) were authorised by an Act of Parliament in 1830 to discourage gin drinking! Any householder could get an excise license to sell beer only, provided he paid two guineas and produced a surety for £20.
It was not named CATCHALL until the 1891 census.

Catchall - Jennifer Paling

"The river which runs through Catchall and under the road eventually ends up at Lamorna. I have heard that the name Catchall came because of a public house situated so they say on the corner on the left as you go up the hill to St Buryan. I remember Mr and Mrs Lawry and Mr and Mrs Hill living in the cottages there. (Mr Hill was killed by a bull at Higher Drift Farm).

We (the Styles family) lived in the house on the corner at Catchall (Westways) – on the right as you travel towards Lands End. We had a room which we called our play room with table tennis and a windup gramophone. We used to play in there. Mother had her hands full with us three children.

This house was previously occupied by the Manager of the milk dairy. This was around the corner about 200 yards towards Lands End.

When we were there the 'factory', as we called it, was used by Cyril Eddy at Trenuggo for storing straw and for occasional whist drives

It was wonderful for us as children and we used to spend quite a lot of time climbing around in the valleys of the roofs.

It was demolished sometime in the late 60s when the corner of the road was altered after a fatality at Catchall.

The people who lived next door to us for most of the time were the Lawrences - 2 brothers and a sister who had retired after running a market garden business

We had no mains electricity until about 1963 before which, like many people, we relied on Tilley lamps, Primus stoves, candles and the Cornish 'slab'. Then a Rayburn cooker and a small generator for electric lights for a while.

We had no mains water until about 1965 when the source of our drinking water, a spring across the road, was condemned as unfit!!

We did have an indoor toilet (though no bathroom) fed by water from the stream pumped by a ram housed in a gully below the Milk dairy.

This amazing water pressurised dome pumped water to the top of our house as well as up to the fields above our house for the animals of Higher Drift farm (Tom Mike Olds).

It did not need any fuel – just a head of water from the stream and could be heard like a beating heart pumping away.

There was a post box on the corner and the Lands End - Penzance bus stopped outside. My eldest brother Michael went to Sancreed school while my younger brother and I started at Tolcarne in Newlyn.

We bought our milk initially from Mr Olds at Higher Drift farm.

Fish was delivered by Mr Collins from Buryas Bridge by horse and cart.

The hunt used to meet regularly on the corner." *Jennifer Paling*

Catchall Dairy Company Limited. Minutes 1889 - 1943

The Company's trademark appears stamped at the commencement of the first book recording the minutes of the Directors meetings in 1891 and was used in the form of a butter stamp up to the introduction of 'National Butter' in 1940 and continued to be used on the Company's letter-heading.

In 1889 T B Bolitho MP approached Mr M Roach of Bejowans, who was one of his tenants, with a view to ascertaining whether the formation of a Farmers' Dairy Company would be supported by the local producers.

Approximately 22 farmers gave their support at the start. More promised to do so later. Mr T B Bolitho generously gave financial assistance, leased local premises at Catchall to the Company and purchased the necessary plant.

Mr H Thomas was appointed Manager of the Company and the directors were Messrs T.Edmonds Higher Leah, J.Pearce Tregonebris, J.Rowe Kerris, M.Roach Bejowens, J.J.Hichens Trenuggo and J.Hollow Treave.

In 1893 a portable steam engine was purchased to replace the water wheel for separating milk, the wheel being retained for pumping of water. Corn grinding was now being undertaken and throughout the years up to 1912 bonuses were paid. (This portable steam engine appears to have been in regular use for over 40 years).

Catchall Dairy and the Sanatogen Company

'Sanatogen', the world~famous nerve tonic, with five other products including Sanatogen wine, was first manufactured one hundred years ago using milk from Catchall Dairy. It was transported in a tank drawn by two horses side by side driven by Phillip John Pengelly of Sancreed.

February 1920 In consequence of the St Just miners' public protest against the local rise in the price of butter as the result of deregulation, Catchall Dairy, Lands End Dairy and Genatson Company (Sanatogen) conferred together as to a joint policy to meet the situation.

As a temporary measure to allay lawlessness the three Companies supplied about 1/2 ton of butter weekly for two weeks to the St Just miners at 2/6d. per lb.

Oct 1933 It was resolved to register under the Milk Marketing Scheme.

1938 Primrose Dairy, having moved to St Erth, sold their Grumbla and Sancreed premises to Catchall Dairy.

May 1939 Catchall Dairy Company moved from the premises at Catchall to their new premises at Grumbla, Sancreed. **(See Grumbla),**

Jan 1943 Catchall Dairy's Good Will and Fixed Assets were sold to Messrs. Cow and Gate.

Managers 1889 H Thomas, 1898 J Hichens, 1901 W J Warren, 1903 G S Nix, 1918 B.Warren, 1933 L J Reynolds, 1934 W E Clook, 1935 J Prowse, 1940 C W Angove, resigned 1943.

HENDRA – meaning 'an old house' – (on the Sancreed/St Buryan boundary) Richard Williams

Richard married in 1940 and lived at Hendra. He worked with his brother William farming Bejowans and Hendra. In 1970, his only son, Tom, married Elizabeth daughter of Revd Eric Hodges Rector of The Lizard. Tom became a teacher.

BEJOWANS

Matthew Roach farmed Bejowans from about 1880 followed by his son William.

Thomas Henry Williams, who was born at Portherris Farm, Pendeen, came to Bejowans with his second wife, Annie nee Badcock, in about 1916/17 from Higher Kemyell. Their four children were Richard, William, Gwen, and Mary. Thomas Henry died in 1939.

John Lutey Williams, his son by his late first wife, immigrated to Australia from Trevean.

Two children drown on farm

A terrible tragedy occurred at Bejowans in January 1945 when Mary, 4 year-old daughter of William and Katherine Williams, fell into a container of boiling water and died in hospital next day. Another tragedy occurred three years later when, in 1948, their 2½ year old only son, Graham James, died in 4 inches of water. The child had been missed for a while and a search was started. After an hour he was found dead in a bin on the farm. His mother and father had been on holiday and returned to learn of the tragedy.

On right William Williams of Bejowans with his elder brothers, John (seated) and Richard.

Top left: Bejowans and above: View from Bejowans.

Alarming incident near St Buryan
Young woman's narrow escape

An alarming incident happened near St Buryan during the thunderstorm on Tuesday night, when a house occupied by Mr. John Lawrey, a workman on Mr. Roach's farm at Bejowans, was struck by lightning and Mr. Lawrey's daughters had an extremely narrow escape from serious injury.

The house, which is situated at the foot of Trelew Hill, is a comparatively modern building. The lightning apparently struck the chimney, a portion of which crashed through the roof and ceiling and fell onto the bed in which Mr. Lawrey's daughters had been sleeping. Fortunately the young women had just left the bed, but Isabel, the youngest, was struck on the head by a falling stone as she was about to pass out of the doorway.

A hole about 6 ft. long was made in the roof, and quite a cartload of debris fell on to the bed and into the room. The remaining portion of the chimney fell into the yard. The lightning appears to have descended the chimney, and forced the stove and the mantelpiece of the sitting-room into the room, smashing the back of the grate.

Naturally Mr. Lawrey and his family were greatly alarmed, but under the circumstances they must consider themselves extremely fortunate that they escaped serious injury. *The Cornishman*

Isabel later married Norman Hosking of Great Sellan who died aged 34 leaving her with seven children and a large farm to run. See Great Sellan Farm.

International Singer at Bejew

At Bejew now lives international singer Sarah McQuaid with her husband and family. Two of her CDs are "I Won't Go Home 'Till Morning", and, with Zoe Young, "Crow Coyote Buffalo."

CHAPTER 3

TRENUGGO House on a cave (There was a cave at Catchall)

FLEW FROM ST BURYAN PARISH TO SANCREED PARISH ON A TRACTOR.
St Buryan man survives 40 ft. crash fall

Eamonn Cocking had a lucky escape on 28 June 1984 when the tractor he was driving burst through a hedge in Trelew Hill, St Buryan and dropped 40ft down onto a field belonging to Trenuggo Farm, Sancreed. The accident took place where the road at the bottom of Trelew Hill, not far from the A30 junction, is built up across the valley on a high embankment.

Eamonn Cocking *"Where I went over, I left St Buryan parish, went over the hedge and landed the other side of the river in Sancreed. It was just an accident really, just one of those things. When the tractor landed it hit a bit of a wall at the bottom and a hedge there. If it had fallen on the other side I would've been under water and I could've been drowned and all that boiling hot oil from the hydraulic tank would've come on me as well, which would have been really nasty."*

Those on the scene who watched the rescue operation estimated it took 1½ hours for the firemen with cutting operations to free the driver Eamonn Cocking from the mangled safety cab of the machine.

Foncene, Eamonn's wife, came upon the accident on her way home from work. *"I had mother with me in the car and we came past it and there were two fire engines on the road there and we drove past them and didn't think it was Eamonn because I knew he was working in St Buryan. We went past it and we met the vicar and Dicky Ruff in the car and my Dad was in the back sitting in between the two seats leaning forward and I could see Dicky Ruff, he pointed at me and I could see him saying "That's her" and soon as he said it I knew it was Eamonn. It was the longest night of our lives. All the hours that night in the waiting room just seemed to go on and on and on. I went in to see him in the morning; he had his leg in traction. And his face, I'll never forget it. He was swollen up like a football. They covered his head where it was fractured but he had little digs and that all over him and purple. He had so much wrong with him they had a hard job to know where to start. He can't remember July at all; it was only August that he started coming around. I didn't think he was going to make it. It's a miracle. Instead of the 6 million dollar man they used to call him the 3 million dollar man."*

As things turned out I'm lucky!

Eamonn, who was in hospital until October with a catalogue of injuries including two fractures to his skull, a broken neck, two or three broken ribs, a broken leg, a smashed knee, a torn oesophagus, a damaged lung punctured by his ribs, a crushed liver and colon amongst other injuries, puts his recovery down to his age and the fact that his farming job kept him fit and healthy plus having the right medical staff to work on him. He also had a very caring wife.

Walking with my dogs kept my joints moving which was a vital part of my recovery.

"As things turned out I'm lucky – things could have turned out much worse, much, much worse. All it would have taken was loss of a limb or something like that, a world of difference between what I am now."

TRELEW/BOJEW HILL 1837

It has been said that in Queen Victoria's coronation year the author's great grandmother, Mary Ann Jacka Cocking, aged 10, riding side saddle, was the first person to ride down Trelew Hill when it was opened in 1837 and on up Bojew Hill.

NB Previously, to travel on the old road, she would have had to turn left 100 yards past the entrance to Trelew Farm, circle the valley and come back on the old road about 100 yards before Trenuggo Gate.

TRENUGGO

This farm was farmed in the 1880s by a man called John Jacka.

He combined this with the position of farm baliff to the late Edward Bolitho. Jacka's tenancy ended about 1886 and James Hitchens, who had farmed at Crowan for the past 30 years, succeeded him as tenant. A Madron man by birth, he was probably pleased to come back to the far west again. Hitchens went on to become a founder member and director at the nearby Catchall Dairy.

The 1891 census shows him the father of 4 girls and 3 boys between the ages of 19 and 32. All then unmarried and all born in Crowan.

James Hitchens' son, also James, followed him as tenant and then for some reason his brother, Christopher, took Trenuggo for about 20 years until 1937. Not one of the children appears to have married and when they attended Sancreed Church on Sundays, they filled all the front pews!

Robert Eddy and family come to Trenuggo

Robert Eddy, his wife Janie, nee Berryman and 3 sons Jack, Claud, and Cyril came to Trenuggo in 1938. Jack went on to farm Lower Leha, (the St Buryan side), and Claud farmed Bone Farm, Madron.

They had come from Bosigran in Zennor where the Eddys had been farming for over 350 years. In the earlier centuries the Eddys were also involved in mining and the 'stamps'. The mine was possibly called Bosigran Consols.

As well as farming, Robert was able to run a very successful cattle-dealing enterprise.

At Bosigran, Zennor, where the Eddy family grew up, the 300ft high cliffs became the training ground for Commandos in the 2nd World War 1939-45. The place is known as Commando Ridge. The Count House at Bosigran (visible from the road) now houses the climbers. Bosigran is now the property of National Trust.

Cyril Eddy & his Shires

"My first recollection of the shire was in 1931 when I was attending Zennor School. It was springtime and the travelling stallion was due in the village for his weekly one night stop, in what was called, "Uncle William's stable".

As children we were warned on no account must we go near the stable but I was already fascinated by the heavy horse and Rex Williams and myself used to go along at breakfast time to feast our eyes on this lovely animal.

Cyril Eddy and his Shires.

In 1945 The Western Area Ploughing Match was inaugurated. There were 103 entries, of which 42 were teams of horses, the majority of which were shires. However, by 1947 the heyday of the working heavy horse was over, as tractors took over on the majority of farms."

For Cyril Eddy it was the beginning of a lifetime of horse ploughing, showing, and other equestrian events, which gave so much pleasure to so many people. He won many cups and other prizes and took great pride in his shire horses. It gave him particular pleasure when the time came that his son Robert and Grandson Jamie could plough with him in the same match.

In recent years, his son Robert has taken up the reins with his carriage driven by 10 shires.

Robert and his Team.

LESBEW

SHEILA HICKS – by Jill Leiworthy (nee Hicks)

"Sheila Cavell Hicks, formerly Warren, was born at Bosliven Farm, St Buryan in 1916. However, tragically, when she was only 3 years old her dear mother, Laura Warren nee Pengelly, died, leaving her and her two older brothers, William and Bernard, with their father, Richard Warren.

It was at this time that she went to live with her Granny and Grandpa Pengelly at Lesbew in Sancreed. Lesbew she said was a magical place and it was here as a child that she played in the woods and by the stream dreamily lost in the wonder and beauty of nature and the mystical world of the nature spirits, which were to appear in her paintings later on. Sheila spoke fondly of trips on Sundays when she loved to go to Sancreed Church with the pony and jingle where she would cuddle under a blanket and eat one of her Granny's delicious saffron buns.

Over the years she spent some of her time with her father but being a very sensitive and delicate child, she was often returned to her gentle grandparents and the magic and solitude of the woods at Lesbew to recover her strength.

In her early teens she lived at St Just for a while with her father and stepmother Bertha. However, when her dear Granny died she was once more packed off to Lesbew to look after her Grandfather. It was a sad and lonely time for her then as a teenager and having left West Cornwall School, it was decided that she should go to the Penzance Art School for 2 or 3 days a week. These days at the art school were the happiest days of her life. She drank in every moment and was taught by the great teacher Mr Lias. It was through this that her talent unfolded and her everlasting passion for painting and that led her to be made a member of the Newlyn Art Gallery where she exhibited her paintings with the great painters of the Newlyn School such as Dame Laura Knight, Lamorna Birch etc while in her early twenties. Still in her early twenties she went on to exhibit at the prestigious Paris Salon – the equivalent of our Royal Academy- and where she exhibited right up until she was 91 in 2007, just before she died.

While she had been living at St Just, she had met Roy Hicks at the midsummer ball but soon after she was whisked away to Lesbew and so she never saw him again………

However, destiny was to take a hand and one day a stray cow appeared at the farm – not being able to find out to whom it belonged Grandpa Pengelly put an advert in the Cornishman and lo and behold who should turn up on his motorbike to collect the cow but Roy Hicks! The rest is history – a few years later they married and went to live at Tregiffian Farm in Sennen and had two daughters. It was at this time that Sheila started painting her babies for which she became famous, since at a stroke she could capture the fragility and innocence of a child.

Later she was to study sculpture with her great friend Barbara Tribe and being a devout Christian she made a sculpture of St Sancreed for the Church, she also restored the head and child of the Madonna and Child at Sennen Church and made a statue of St Buriana for St Buryan Church to name but a few.

She was a mystic and philosopher and well versed in classical music, poetry and literature as well as being a most talented artist for which she was recognised and proudly made a Cornish Bard – named Artist of Cornwall."

For Sheila
Formed in the womb by moor, sea and sky
In times when death was the casual passer-by.
Born to the land of mystery, song and dance
Where soon you found your chosen place.
A girl's soul eye was quick to see
The edge of life no fearful place to be.
In fields of green and steadfast granite,
Where more than earthly creatures inhabit,
Your deeper sight saw magic weave and way
Ethereal companions joining you in play.

Overseen by sunrise sky and sunset tide
Your seasons passed, your choices made.
You imagined love in shades of fame and blue,
Though all colours seem the same not all of them are true.
Through the gift of birth, its burdens and its bliss,
Two souls you bore to the land of gentle mist.

A restlessness within you stirred
The angel whispers the girl once heard
Spoke again and again and would not go
"Use your gift; capture this unequalled glow".
Then how the canvass filled with life and light
Stirred by voices beyond our sight,
When child, or flower or cloud take form
As in the eye of a heavenly storm,
Where colour breaks free to flow and dance
And forms emerge as if by chance.

So many of these expansive flows
Were filled with meditations hours;
Your faith and wonder at God's creation
Honed your skills and inspiration.
You painted love and loved to paint
And on these tokens your love was spent.

Larry

Eulogy for John Eddy   by Robert Eddy

"John Eddy was born at Lesbew farm to John and Olga Eddy. He had two sisters both younger than him, Mary and Cathy.

John first attended school at Sancreed. Other people that attended at the same time as John were William and Tommy James, Desmond Nicholls, Jeffrey and Susan Taylor and Michael Adams.

I said to Desmond Nicholls, "John wasn't that religious" to which Desmond immediately replied, "But he never did anyone any harm". That is the basis of a religion I suppose. John, like all farmers' children at the time, had certain chores to do before he walked across the fields to school nearly a mile away with muddy boots. John would be promptly taken to the class next door and have his leg slapped. Next day the boots would be the same. John's party trick at school was to be able to bend a 6 inch nail, the only child able to do so. He had physical strength and strength of character.

Probably, John's closest pal was Jesse Thomas, brother of Anita George of Tregonebris farm, a neighbouring farm to Lesbew. One winter Alfred Olds's irrigation quarry pool froze - Ice road truckers have got nothing on John and Jesse, they decided to ride their bikes on it and John's bike went through the ice!

John started working full time for Donald Payne in St Just. He was going there the morning he had his terrible accident. It was the same time as his middle sister Mary was giving birth to John's nephew, Bobby. John was not expected to survive the accident it took him 5 years to recover, three and a half years of it in plaster. During that time he could be regularly seen on his Fordson Major along with plaster cast and crutches.

John's first job after his accident was at Trenuggo. Going up Treganares I was driving and looking over the hedge trying to wave at Desmond Nicholls mowing the grass. I lost control of the lorry and we went into the ditch. All I could think of was I've smashed John up again. The lorry went up the hedge and flopped over on its side in the middle of the road. John came down on top of me. I scrambled out through the passenger window, stood on the ground, looked through the windscreen and there was John-head down, feet in the air wedged between the steering wheel and the seat. All I was shouting was "come on before it catches fire". John eventually struggled and got on his feet but he didn't get out then. He proceeded to rummage through the loose material in the cab until he found his crib bag, he checked his flask to see if it was broke before passing it to me, and then he climbed out. I ran out to tell father, who was milking at the time, I said "Quick I've turned the lorry over up Tregonares". He said "What you doing here?" I said, "Well I'm not old enough to be driving it am I?" It was ok though, by the time we got back to the lorry, John was well in control and had started to organise recovery, and dealt with the police as well.

Later John drove for Hitchens transport and met his wife Margaret. John was 33 Margaret was 27 when they were married. They spent the first two years of their marriage living and working from Lesbew while they had a house built in Heamoor. John couldn't wait to show me. It was his pride and joy. Margaret is still living there. They had two children Helen and John Francis. When JF was 10 months old he ended up in South

Mead hospital with kidney problems. Margaret stayed with the child in hospital for 3 weeks. Hitchens transport arranged for John to shunt trailers to Bristol, which enabled John to visit Margaret and JF practically every day. After which he was taken back every fortnight for 6 months. Needless to say, JF is now 27 and living life to the full, and his sister Helen has given John two grandchildren – Robin and George, who I knew John was very proud of.

John, after his accident, and his youngest sister getting killed at 21 and now his son in South Mead hospital must have wondered what more life was going to throw at him.

He knocked his bad leg on steel when he was loading. While he was away his leg poisoned and things steadily got worse, it got so bad that before he got home, he had to be lifted out of his cab with a forklift. Margaret looked at his leg and said "John you'll have to go to the hospital with that". "No" said John I'll have a bath and go bed and it will be all right in the morning. His brother-in-law Robert Williams came to visit him that night. Margaret sent him upstairs to see John. The next thing she heard was Robert shouting at John, "you are going to have to get out of the bed to go to hospital now". An action which at least saved his life. Eventually John had to have the bottom of his leg amputated.

Lorry drivers do not have anything to aspire to – like stripes or medals – but
If lorry drivers were boxers – John would have been a champ,
If lorry drivers were athletes – John would have been a gold medallist
If lorry drivers were politicians – John wouldn't have achieved very much as he was too honest, but John was respected and admired by his fellow drivers."

TREGONEBRIS Treganebris 1331
Tre + Conebris = The settlement of Cunebris

The Marracks of Tregonebris
From notes of Capt. John RN & Peter Alexander-Marrack

There was a Marten 'Marrak' living in the parish of Paul as early as 1522, and there were Marracks farming at Castallack around 1600 and from at least the 1690's and throughout much of the 18th century.

The first Marrack venture into the parish of Sancreed was in 1710 with a lease of part of Trevean.

For many years it was a widespread Marrack family belief that "the Marracks had been at Tregonebris since the time they lived in caves and painted themselves with woad". However, we now know that the connections of

THE COTTAGE TREGONEBRIS SANCREED WEST CORNWALL.

the Marrack family with Tregonebris only began in the late 1750s and lasted until about 1870. In addition, various Marracks held land in Higher Drift and Lower Drift and in Boswarthen.

There were three farms at Tregonebris.

TREGONEBRIS, the southern farm formerly **The Manor Farm**

In the 18th and 19th centuries, the Manor was limited to the southern farmland held by the Buller family and leased by one branch of the Marrack family. Two maps (the 1789 map in CRO item BU/1176 and the 1839 Tithe Apportionment map (CRO FTM 205) clearly show that the associated farmhouse was situated on the south side of the lane, in the grounds of the present 1875 house which has replaced it.

Philip Marrack 1705–1787 + Duence Hoskin leased the Southern farm in 1759.

Their son Richard 1749–1821 + Joan Permewan leased it in 1787.

Philip 1799–1862 + Anna Hodge leased it in 1821.

Philip 1829–1865 + Mary Hockin leased it in 1859 and "Bibliotheca Cornubiensis" of 1874 records that his brother, Richard Marrack, (1831-1890, the well-known Truro solicitor) was born at the Manor House, Tregonebris.

From 1890s this farm was let to Richard & John Tremaine Pearce.

The southern farm was farmed from the 1930s until 1971 by John Pengelly and then by his son William until 1980.

The Pengelly Tree

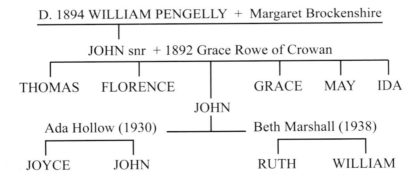

The Pengelly Connection

Up to the mid 1800s William Pengelly with his wife Margaret had been farming at Higher Botrea. They were planning to emigrate to USA when Boscawenoon, St Buryan was offered them. They felt that this tenancy of 107 acres was too good an offer to miss. Their son John was only eight at this time.

When John Pengelly Snr. grew up he courted Grace Rowe of Crowan, travelling perhaps 13 miles each way on horseback. His persistence was rewarded for they married in 1892. When his father William died in 1894 John Snr. took over the farm. They had six children Thomas, Florence, Grace, May, John, and Ida.

In 1928, the two sons Tom and John Jnr with their father cleared and prepared the Boscawenoon circle, an ancient site. **This was for the first modern Bardic ceremony of the Cornish Gorsedd. Crowds of people journeyed to Boscawenoon to witness a spectacle that had not been seen there for 1000 years!** Of the family, May and Ida married bank managers, Tom with his sisters Florence and Grace did not marry and remained at Boscawnoon. Their father died in 1930 and in that

The Pengelly house at Tregonebris.

year John Pengelly Jnr. married Ada Hollow of Treave, St Buryan and took over a farm at Tregonebris. They had two children Joyce in 1932 and John Douglas in 1934.

On the 5th of March 1935 Ada, (out in the garden with her two small children), died suddenly and was found by the workman. She was only 29.

Joyce and John Douglas were invited to spend the war years in Canada, but fortunately they did not go. The ship they were to have sailed on was sunk by German U-boats! It was fortunate for me, for later I married Joyce!!

John Pengelly remarried and chose his wife's school friend Beth Marshall from Polperro in 1938 and they had two children Ruth and William.

On 6th Sept 1941 two para mines dropped and exploded in grass fields at Tregonebris. As the bombs fell Joyce dived under the bedclothes as glass shattered and covered her bed. Her father came in and said, "Don't move". He gathered up the counterpane with the glass and threw it out of the window. Almost all of the windows in the house were smashed and the roof was badly damaged. Their neighbour, Mrs Thomas, also had her greenhouse destroyed and her front door crashed in. There was considerable damage to the farm buildings. Apparently a bomb dropped near a water tank which had a galvanised roof. They never found the roof. The tank was still full of water next day! A policeman called to check if they were all right, and possibly for some tea and sympathy!

On the same night two more para mines were dropped; one in the woods at Trewidden Estate, the other demolished the Tregavera Methodist Chapel nearby.

TREGONEBRIS, the northern farm

From before 1900 this was farmed, by Robert, Jesse, and then Percival Thomas.
In 1919 Percy Thomas, Jesse's brother, was killed while flying in Hampshire.

Anita George nee Thomas

Someone who, in her lifetime so far, has shown considerable versatility and a talent for helping others in the various fields of education, sport, civic duties and fund-raising activities,amongst others, is Anita George.

Born at Tregonebris, in the blizzard of February 1947, Anita Margaret Thomas, as she then was, was the daughter of Percival Jesse Thomas and his Belgian wife, the former Miss Adrienne Van Vossell who had fled Belgium to find safety in Cornwall. Her passage in a fishing boat, which landed in Newlyn, would have been truly terrifying during war time with no knowledge of her destination. The Thomas family had farmed at Tregonebris for several generations. When Anita was a child growing up here there were no modern conveniences in the farmhouse. Rooms were lit at night by paraffin oil lamps. There was no modern sanitation, or electricity, no bathroom and a special stove heated bath water

At an early age, Anita learned to milk the cows by hand using a bucket and stool.

Milk was strained into churns and transported by Will Hattam to Sancreed dairy. Besides milking Anita helped out with seasonal crops, hoeing mangels and with the hay and corn harvests.

Threshing day dinners were served on a very large table in Granny's kitchen, Granny being Bessie Thomas nee Stevens. The meal consisted of boiled beef and carrots and rice pudding.

Anita was taught at Sancreed Church of England primary school by Mrs Greaves and her daughter Phyllis. They lived in the house attached to the school. These teachers were followed by a Mrs Thomas from Wales and Miss Pat Rowe (The late Mrs Douglas Reynolds). These were happy days followed by attending Penzance Grammar school for girls. Here Anita was able to excel in music and sport. Her music teacher was Mrs Fitkin, the wife of the vicar of Sancreed. Hockey and putting the shot were both sports at which Anita attained proficiency.

Another unusual achievement for which Anita became well known was the fact that a beautiful childhood photograph of her was the one chosen to appear on the biscuit tin of Furniss the Cornish biscuit firm based at Truro; the picture would eventually adorn thousands of biscuit tins to be exported to countries all round the world.

On leaving school Anita made her career with Whitaker and Redfearn the Penzance accountants, and then at Barclays Bank. She represented the latter at tennis, hockey and netball.

In 1967 she became a finalist for the title of Dairy Queen of Great Britain. This meant travelling to Woburn Abbey with 14 other finalists, and being entertained most lavishly as Dairy Princesses by the Duke and Duchess of Bedford.

For many years before her marriage Anita played the organ at Sancreed church and at St Just on occasions, where she sang in the choir.

On her marriage to Peter George, a farming family, she joined the choir at St Buryan church. Anita's first involvement with cricket was in 1970 and to this day SHE remains secretary of the West Penwith Evening League.

During the 70s Anita spent most of her time bringing up her family of two boys and helping her husband Peter run the haulage business; driving a lorry herself for about two years.

In 1982 Peter, Anita and family moved to the Logan Rock Inn at Treen, where they have enjoyed 25 successful years.

Anita can count over 30 public and charitable appointments associated with her.

Perhaps the most significant is that of a Bench Chairman of West Cornwall Magistrates.

Delineated in what is now termed a CV are a great many appointments as chairman, treasurer, trustee, school governor, committee member and so on to a wide spectrum of societies.

Cricket of course features high on the list, as Anita became the first lady to be elected to the Cornwall County Cricket Club in 1996. Her sons, Nicholas and Mark are County Cricket players and her husband Peter is very well known in cricketing circles.

Health authority matters and St Buryan school governor, together with that special "first" again, that of lady Rotarian of the Penzance club in 2007, make up some of Anita's other accomplishments. Her biggest accolade was to be awarded the MBE in 2008 in the New Year's Honours List.

In 2004, Peter and Anita acquired the Yacht Inn on the Promenade; which has become a popular venue aand more recently the King's Arms at Paul Churchtown.

Her father Percival Jesse Thomas farmed at Tregonebris. His brother Bernard Thomas farmed Anjarden, and later lived at Newton Ferrers. His sister Mary married Enoch Pengelly from Toldavas and went to live at a farm near Porthpean, St Austell. Both are deceased.

TREGONEBRIS, the western farm,

The former old farmhouse has become a farm cottage now for many years. It was named in the Penwith "Listed Buildings" tabulation as the "old manor house" which appears to be incorrect as the land around that property was not the manor land.

Up to 1930 this farm was occupied for many years by John Tremaine Pearce followed by John Pengelly who soon after moved into the southern farm. From that time the western farm became a farm cottage.

ROSMERGY – a Tregonebris farm cottage on the A30

Arson at Rosemergy

On 27th April 1961, John Robert Miller of no fixed abode was charged with maliciously setting fire to the cottage Rosmergy in Sancreed. Let to Mr John Pengelly it is alleged that he had started four fires to cover up the fact that he had spent the night there. Miller had reported it to the police himself when he became very concerned. Mr Percy Matthews, the previous occupier had only moved to another house on that day.

Apparently there had been a case of death possibly by arson at Rosemergy many years previous.

GOLDHERRING

The Iron Age settlement at Goldherring was excavated by archeologists between 1958 – 62. This 'Round' built initially in the first century AD, and containing smallish round houses, was set in a block of small rectangular fields. Traces of barley, wild or cultivated oats, and rye had been found there. These indicated arable farming.

Goldherring was also the site of a very early smelting works.

It was first mentioned as a separate holding in the 1839 tithes. Goldherring had formerly been an outlying part of the northern Tregonebris farm.

In 1845 when Alexander Rowe Marrack died, Goldherring was excluded from the sale. Marrack's six daughters Caroline, Nanny, Mary Ann, Eliza, Emily, and Elizabeth Marrack inherited it.

Goldherring was sold to Thomas Bedford Bolitho in the mid 1860s. Around this time it was occupied by, among others, Mary & William Williams, William Clemens (miner), & William Trezise (miner).

Chris Matthews, Newshop

William Christopher Matthews (Chris Matthews) born at St Just was a miner in 1881 at the age of 17 years. Soon after he moved to Goldherring and became a carpenter by trade. By 1891 he had moved his flourishing business to Newshop, St Buryan. The 1914 Kelly's directory stated that William Christopher Matthews was a carpenter, builder, contractor, wheelwright, house decorator and undertaker at Newshop and Sennen. He was also a moneylender. The firm that started from small beginnings at Goldherring well over 100 years ago, has built many houses, and has now developed into a large and successful business.

William John Hosken

William John Hosken came to farm Goldherring from Chyangwens, St Buryan, when he married Fanny Stone in 1929. They farmed there for 45 years and had one daughter Eileen who married Vincent Harvey of Boscean, St Buryan.

LOWER LEHA

Deed

Mr Wm Boase to Mary Foss. 14 Apr 1787.

Lease for 99 years on the lives of Mary Foss (party), Will Foss her son, Eliz Foss her daughter, of 5 acres of Crofts in Tregonebris etc (near Leha Vean). Consideration: to erect a house. Yearly rent: 25s 0d; Herriot 2s 6d. Witnessed by Willm Carne and Harper.

Billy Foss the poet from William Bottrell

In 29 Feb 1824, Mary Foss having died, the property at what is now Lower Leha in Sancreed Parish, was leased to her son Billy Foss.

Billy Foss, nicknamed 'Frost' was one of the personalities who made his presence felt by entertaining the locals in and around St Just, Sancreed and other local places with his impromptu skits and chimney-corner tales in the first half of the 19th century. However it was by his longer tales, known as 'drolls' that had entertained many generations before he was born that he made a chief contribution to local culture, carrying on the work of the old local bards. Both William Bottrell and Robert Hunt owed him a debt for the many stories he had told which they had been able to record.

At Tregonebris was living at that time one George Hosking who, though a man of such ability as to have been called on to prepare the Tithe Map in 1838-9 and to have been regarded as an authority on local land matters, was reported as anything but an exemplary husband. His cat in its wanderings once found its way to Billy's cottage, and was sent home with this message tagged on at its neck: -

"Mister George Hosking, your cat is come home
You sent her all over the world for to roam
Take her again, now, and spare her sweet life
Banish your keep-miss and take back your wife."

Billy's chief occupation was clock cleaning, but he was always called on for any odd job that needed ingenuity, and besides being able to roll off an extempore rhyme on any occasion, would entertain the whole household by reciting in rhyme from memory while his jobs were in hand. He also cut milestones. Billy Foss's greatest effort in this direction is seen at Crows-an-wra. The milestone there is considered the most ornate in Cornwall. During the War it was buried and all signposts were removed when invasion was expected!

One corn harvest, it seems, Billy helped a Buryan farmer to make up a few round arish-mows in a field near the highway, and some mischievous boys, after playing pranks there, taunted him with the rhyme: -

"As I was walking on the road I saw a mow fell all abroad:
I'm sorry for the farmer's loss- The mow was made by Billy Foss."

Billy gave them as good in return:-

"The mow was made, and all complete; It was a splendid mow of wheat.
The rogues and thieves in Buryan Ch'town Stole the sheaves, and the mow fell down."

As Billy once passed through Buryan Cburchtown one day, a wag cried to him,

"Billy Foss is at a loss In tolling of the bell!"

Billy threw back;-

"There's not a man in Buryan Ch'town Can toll the bell so well!"

One day Billy was surprised by a well-known voice behind him; the voice of one of whom he expected more courtesy, hailing him as "Old Frost and Snow." Turning round he said:-

"Very early in the spring, I heard a cuckoo for to sing;
His voice was very soft and low, Singing bitter, bitter, 'Frost and Snow.'"

Billy had a musical ear almost as remarkable as his for "setting clocks a-working after all the goldsmiths Penzance had given them up"; he could at once name any musical note that he heard, and led the Sancreed church singers with a hautboy (oboe), one of the few specimens of instrument then in the district. Specimens of his slate-carving may still be seen, one in Zennor and another close to the gate at Madron Church. Doubtless much of his lettering decorates other stones which he did not trouble to sign with his name.

In Sancreed parish there was also living a travelling tailor, one Lewis Grenfell. To Billy Foss he said:-

"You go up an' down from country to town,
Cutting letters in wood and in stone;
By your trade, though, you lose, for it won't find you shoes,
And as for best clothes, you have none!"

Billy retorted;-

"I'm honest, at least, for I still pay my debt:
That's more than a tailor or miller's done yet!"

One of his best and most-quoted rhymes was that of Balleswidden Mine, St Just, relating the history of difficulties overcome there. Here is one verse;-

"And then they had an inyin (engine) good, That draa'd the water like a flood,
And sucked right up the very mud Of the Mine of Balleswidden!"

LOWER LEHA

Farmer in the making

For about 20 years up to 1957 Lower Leha was farmed by Fred Trezise. He had a deformed leg caused by accident at Lesbew a few years earlier. He was followed by John Clegg from Stockport, Cheshire. While still at school Henwood Thomas helped the latter on the farm and later became the farmer himself, now living in St Buryan village.

CHAPTER 4

BRANE AREA

Murder

David Try: "In 1890 two brothers, John Oats aged about 33 and Edwin Oats about 32, living at Brane, had a fight in a field there and John died. Edwin ended up in Broadmoor, registered as a lunatic, having killed his brother John. Family folklore has it that they were working in the fields when an argument broke out resulting in a fight to the death. He spent the rest of his life in Broadmoor."

The inquest was held in the Brane Bible Christian chapel where their father had been a steward. An older married brother testified that Edwin had suffered stinging pains in the head, arms and legs during the last 12 or 15 months. He had been to his doctors – Mr Searle, Mr Montgomery, Mr Dodge and Mr Fox. They all said it was rheumatism and gave him pills. "Edwin and John were on affectionate terms. I believe that either would have laid down his life for the other".

The Cornishman reports that after the arrest, the sergeant and constable with their prisoner, stopped off at Drift at the undertaker's shop on their way to Penzance police station to give an order for the coffin!

GEAR BRANE

Rodney Hutchings

"My father and mother moved to Gear Brane in 1956 with their two children, myself and Rodney Hutchings, aged seven years old, and my sister June who was five and a half. Our first four cows (Ivy, Ruby, Starry and Nellie) came from my uncle Lawrence, who farmed at Higher Bollogus, Drift. We had some sows and 150 deep litter chickens and 2 acres of early potatoes. My dad, Wesley Hutchings, had a threshing set, threshing on local farms and several in the St Erth area.

A man called Jack Phillips from Grumbla worked with my father on threshing day. He really loved the job. In 1943 they acquired Mr Reynold's threshing machine, a 'Marshall' with a separate trusser and a really super compound traction engine called 'Westward Ho'. Wesley threshed with it until 1946 when an 'International' tractor was acquired, which threshed at many farms in Paul parish.

Wesley Hutching's threshing machine.

The traction engine was used at Penzance railway sidings for tarmacing, after which Wesley drove it to Holmans foundry in St Just. As he drove into the main entrance, the boiler blew. It was scrapped, having proved a worthwhile investment.

In the late fifties in Sancreed, there was a school, church, chapel, men's institute, milk dairy, riding school, foxhounds owned by Mr Oats, and a cricket club.

Catchall Dairy at Grumbla was the centre of the village. The local farmers brought their milk to the factory quite early and would queue in an assortment of vehicles including tractors and trailers, vans and cars, and sometimes Raymond Bray would arrive with his horse and trap, all before 9.30am when the milk lorries started to arrive. There was a small fleet of five lorries and the drivers waiting their turn to unload would have a cup of tea and scone in the small canteen. My grandfather, JA Hutchings, ran three of the lorries, hauling milk from Paul, St Buryan, St Levan and the Sennen area. Two of his drivers were Clifford and Bernard Hutchings, my uncles. The other two lorries were individually owned by Will Hattam and Jim Roberts, hauling from St Just and Pendeen. A lot of the milk was made into butter. There was also a drying plant for making milk powder. The huge chimneys pouring black smoke at certain times of the day could be seen from miles away. The dairy was once a hive of activity and it was such a shame to see it close in 1962.

Shoot up at the Vicarage. "That's all right then", said the policeman

I remember one summer there were hundreds of crows and rooks in Sancreed village. The vicar got fed up with all the squawking noise. He asked Geoffrey Rowe (Jethro) and me if we would get rid of some of them. He said perhaps with a quiet gun? A few days later Jethro and I turned up with an air gun each. After about an hour we had shot about 40 of them. The noise the survivors made was unbelievable. As we made our way out of the vicarage, there standing at the gate was the local policeman, complete with bicycle. He wanted to know what we were doing. After we explained about the crows and rooks, he then wanted to know if we were old enough to carry guns. We replied we thought so. The policeman said, "Well that's all right then", and walked with us up over Sancreed Beacon. He then went on his way!

In 1959, Sancreed Beacon caught fire. It was so dry that, despite the efforts of the fire brigade and lots of local volunteers, it burned for many weeks. Geoffrey Rowe and I made our own fire beaters and helped out in the evenings. We must have been 11 or 12 years old. That's something that wouldn't happen today.

Wesley Hutchings buys a plane

In 1967, my father Wesley Hutchings was a member of the Land's End Gliding Club and there he met Richard Barnes, (Dick as we called him). As time went on both of them thought of getting a cheap aircraft between them. Eventually they found a four seater, a Miles Messenger, advertised in *Flight* magazine. So Dad got the owner to fly to Land's End airfield. The owner gave Dad and Dick a flight around West Penwith. While they were in the air, Dad asked what the plane was like for landing in small fields. "Excellent", the man said. So Dad asked him if he could land in "that field", pointing to an eight-acre field at Gear Brane with electricity cables at both ends. They managed to land in the field but in doing so punctured one of the tyres, which meant he could not take off again. So Dad offered him about three quarters of the asking price and the train fare home, which he accepted.

When JA Hutchings retired the milk lorries operated from Gear Brane up until we sold the farm in 1971. Milk churn collection slowly dwindled away until in 1978, it gave way to bulk milk collection with tankers."

Rodnet Hutchings and Dick Barnes with Wesley's plane.

BRANE

My father's connection with Brane ... Emma Slack (nee. Glossop)

"Silas Glossop (1902-1993), born in Bakewell, Derbyshire where his father was the bank manager.

Went to Imperial College, London, to study Mining Engineering.

Came down to Pendeen for two summer vacations from university on a motorbike and worked at Levant. He later had connections with the Camborne School of mines. Later he was involved with the mending of the sea floor at Levant."

(This meant pouring cement under water to plug a hole in Levant Mine).

"Student friends with artist John Tunnard of Lamorna and on a New Year visit there in the 60s he and my mother Sheila saw the bungalow at Brane was for sale.

Silas was very amusing and kind, he was very well read.

Later they moved across the road to the farmhouse. They loved West Penwith, its people, landscape and wildlife. They felt welcome and comfortable there and spent the rest of their lives at Brane".

Bill Watters – born St Just 1904, died Plymouth 1997 by Mary Watters

Bill's father, William Abraham Watters, worked in mines in South Africa and in Michigan with his two brothers. He married Ellen Olds of St Just in 1903. They moved to Brane and bought a farm – one of the five mixed farms in a hamlet consisting of a chapel and cottages. He died in 1940 from phthisis, a miner's complaint.

Bill attended Sancreed School and I am led to believe that he was the first pupil to pass the 11+ examination there.

He remembered the artist, Stanhope Forbes, sitting in the lane leading to Sancreed school painting Sancreed Church. I have seen the painting at an exhibition in Penlee Gallery, Penzance but I believe it to be in private hands.

Further education was not an option for Bill, as he was needed on the farm at that time. Later he travelled and his first taste of freedom was a spell in Canada in the 1920s. His friend, Nelson Dennis from Brane Moor, had emigrated to Canada, so Bill worked his passage from Liverpool, looking after cattle who were also emigrating!

He came back because of his father's illness and took over the farm. He married Vashti Warren of St Buryan in 1931 and they had one daughter, Mary, born in 1940.

In the Second World War, assistance on the farm was provided by Land Army girls and various prisoners of war. Bill built a bungalow on his land in Brane in the 1940's. Both he and his father served on local councils in their time and Bill also served as a Methodist local preacher.

The family moved away from Brane in 1950 and settled in Devon. One of Bill Watters proudest moments as President of the Plymouth Cornish Association was to travel back home to welcome his old school friend, a son of Grumbla, Jimmy Remphrey, at the end of his charity walk from John O' Groats to Land's End.

The majority of the land around the hamlet of Brane has been acquired by the Wherry family, who live there, formerly well-known for their Guernsey herd; they are now into beef production.

Brane Bible Christian Chapel

William Rowe of Cardinney, St Buryan and his brother, Michael Rowe of Bolankin, St Buryan with others were the means of the erection of Brane Chapel in about 1845. Before this time there had been a Meetinghouse and a class there.

Situated at the bottom of the lane up to Carn Euny and not far from the Holy Well, the chapel was built on a quiet corner plot, out of sight of the hamlet.

Easter was a special time at this chapel. On Easter Monday there would be a public tea and later a visiting chapel choir would render a *Service of Song*. The chapel, which had seats for 108 people, had regular services until about 1970 when it closed. It is now a private house.

Brane – the White family

Jessie (nee Mason) and Edward White moved to Brane to farm after their marriage in 1888. As well as being man and wife they were also stepbrother and stepsister. Jessie's mother (Jane Mason nee Hosken) died young and so did Edward's father, also called Edward White. The remaining parents, Amos Mason and Jane White (nee Roberts) married and farmed at Bolankin, St Buryan, approximately one mile across the fields from Brane as the crow flies.

Edward and Jessie White had three sons, Edward Thomas, Amos Mason and John Eva who all became farmers.

Edward and John married two of the Hattam sisters from Botrea, May and Gertrude. They met at Trevarthen Chapel, both families being very religious. Edward and May moved to Hendra in Cot Valley to farm and John and Gertrude firstly farmed Brane and then moved to Botrea when Gertrude's parents, Henry and Mary Jane Hattam, retired in 1930. Amos, who married Margaret Jeffery, moved back to Bolankin and took over the farm there from his grandfather, Amos Mason.

Amos and Margaret's only son, Leonard Edward Charles White married Christiana (Chrissie) Wallis from New Mill, daughter of John and Mary Wallis of Tredinnick.

Leonard and Chrissie's first home was a small farm in Brane before moving back to farm Bolankin where their family still farm today.

Edward Thomas White's Diary for 1912.

Edward Thomas White kept a farming diary for the year 1912, which has survived. It shows how the earth was treated and with what (caustic lime, salt, and sand from Sennen Cove), the crops that were grown at Brane (potatoes, turnips, mangolds, corn, cabbages, grass, hay and carrots), the names of the fields and even gives an account of what the local blacksmith's was used for, including repair of boots for his younger brother John! They also kept a bull, cows, pigs, including a sow, which was used on other farms, and poultry, as well as the working horses used for ploughing and at least one pony to pull a trap.

Life was obviously hard with Edward working a full six days a week but Sunday was strictly observed as a day of rest, notwithstanding that he taught at Crows-an-wra and Brane Sunday Schools and in the evening attended Trevarthen Chapel.

However, the diary shows there were excursions with the Band of Hope, attending the Royal Cornwall Show and various outings for Sancreed Tea and Feast, Madron Feast and St Just Feast, as well as trips to collect salt, lime and coal from Newlyn, sand from Sennen Cove, pigs taken to Penzance station and visits to the blacksmiths and the local mill.

Jenkin and Wherry

Clifford Jenkin grew up at Bunkers Hill, St Buryan, the eldest of 5 brothers and 1 sister.

Taking the 17-gallon churns of milk to Catchall Milk Factory he met up with Esther Williams who worked in the office there and who lived in Catchall. Her mother, born 1881, who also worked there, was the eldest of 12 children. Esther and Clifford were married in 1928 and took on a little farm in Brane. They had 3 daughters Eileen, Heather, and Pat.

Eileen Wherry nee Jenkin: " We were all born in Brane, 4 children, 3 girls and a boy. He died at 18 months old when I was nearly 5. We left Brane in 1936 for Tredinney. 14 years later in 1950 we came back there again on another farm.Carn Euny years ago was very overgrown. You had to find your way in through the gorse bushes. In the 1930s there was no signs displayed. If anybody came in Brane who were really interested in archaeology, they would enquire but it was difficult to explain. Willie my husband, as a boy, has taken a lot of people up there for half a crown, and my cousin Muriel Jenkin used to do the same.

Melville & Trevor Wherry in fogue Carn Euny.

Carn Euny was sold in 1950 to The National Trust by Willie's father Henry Wherry, for £50. Ernie Bowles, who was working for my father (Clifford), cut the gorse bushes and cleared it out completely.

It cut off the leg of his bed

On the morning of August Bank Holiday in 1939 there was a terrific thunderstorm. It struck the aerial of Bill Waters' house. It cut the leg off his bed. His father was there ill at the time. He died soon after. Bill's pigs also were killed. Bill said that had he not been in the stable with the horses he would have been killed as well.

Aunt Clara Jenkin, who was 'expecting', came rushing in to Willie's mother. She was terrified.

At Brane Chapel, Clifford played the organ alternating with Henry Wherry .

Henry Wherry from Little Sellan farmed at Brane from the early 1920s. His daughter Hilda married Percy Nicholls of Higher Drift, and his son Willie, in 1953, married the girl next door- me! Melville was born in 1954."

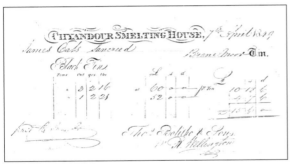

Smelting Docket.

Mining

In the census of 1841, Brane was a mining and farming village. By 1891 there were 58 people living at Brane in 16 houses with 10 houses unoccupied but no miners.

All over Sancreed on so many of the farms are remains of old workings, old shafts, tin stamps etc. In this parish and downstream in neighbouring parishes much surface tin has also been streamed.

Jim Remphrey
END TO END John O'Groats to Lands End (extracts from his book)

"As one of a family of eight children, I was born in the small farming village of Brane, in the Parish of Sancreed, approximately four and a half miles west of Penzance, Cornwall and five and a half from Land's End.

My late parents were of the strong 'Cornish Methodist' type, my father a Methodist lay preacher for about 60 years, and until the latter years of his life he always walked to his preaching appointments, so that according to his records had walked nearly 2000 miles during his preaching life.

This passion for walking seemed to have been passed on to me. Mostly we walked, but once a year we were taken to Marazion on horse drawn wagons by way of Sunday school outings and that was almost like going 'abroad'.

I was employed as a farm labourer and gardener until voluntarily I joined HM Forces, serving in the Royal Engineers in October 1940, and was sent to Greece very early in 1941. I was taken POW by the Germans after about six weeks. After nearly five years of survival as a POW I returned to England in May 1945 – Sancreed's one and only Prisoner of War.

In September 1959, I joined Listers in Dursley and remained there ever since.
From an early age I was fond of singing and sang solos in the local chapels from the age of six and this love of singing has remained with me.

The Great Decision

We have often heard of some one taking on the adventurous walk from Land's End to John O'Groats or vice versa and the daring enterprise fascinated me. To my knowledge, this marathon walk had never then been done by any person born or residing in the Penwith area. Fortunately for me, one particular and lifelong friend whom I had contacted possessed a small caravan and readily expressed his willingness to accompany me."

Extract from *The Dursley Gazette*: *Mr Remphrey said he chose Cancer Research (as his charity) because cancer affects almost everybody. He expects to raise about £3800. The walk will be made in Mr Remphrey's holidays from RA Listers where he works as a storekeeper. He is covering all the expenses out of his own pocket, except that a friend from Cornwall, Mr Stephen Berriman, will accompany him with a car and caravan to supply overnight accommodation). (Stephen's family had farmed at Roskennal Mills.) He added with a smile, "I am getting a thorough medical check-up before I start, though after I may need a post-mortem."*

John o Groats walker Jim Remphrey with his sister Gladys Gendall.

Jim was well equipped with boots and socks and all necessary supplies for the journey, which began on 29th April 1974. As he progressed through England he was supported generously, particularly by the CANCER committees and was walking 25 and more miles a day in spite of continual health problems.

Unfortunately these health issues landed Jim in hospital and it was to be May 10th 1975 before he was able to continue his great walk from where he had left off the previous year.

Jim walked every inch of the road from John O'Groats to Land's End; eight hundred and seventy odd miles and was joined on the last stage of his walk by his sister, Gladys. He was met at Penzance by the Mayor Mr David Pooley, who gave him a cheque and the honour of signing the Distinguished Visitors Book. Also at Penzance he was delighted to meet an old friend from Brane, Bill Watters, who was then the Chairman of Plymouth Cornish Association and had travelled from Plymouth especially to see Jim at the completion of his journey.

"Eventually I arrived at Drift and a group of villagers, mostly old friends, cheered me on. At Catchall I was intercepted when a small car pulled up and out jumped a

school-day friend who brought me some food which I devoured climbing Tregonebris Hill. For the next mile I was able to see, in the distance, the old village of Brane.

At Sennen Post Office, former neighbours Morley and Eira gave me a welcome cheer. I then carried right on to the Land's End Hotel where I was met by Mr Donald Trewern, Chairman of the new Penwith District Council, in his chain of office, who presented me with a plaque .

With about 30 friends I was entertained to tea with Mr Trewern at the nearby hotel with my sisters

Alfred and Norah Olds took Gladys and myself back to her home at Sancreed. This ended a day of great rejoicing for us.

It was almost incredible to think I had now covered every inch of the road from John O'Groats to Lands End; eight hundred and seventy odd miles thus achieving my dreams".

Gladys Gendall sister of Jim Remphrey

My father, John Charles Remphrey tried unsuccessfully to get a farm at Brane. He moved to Chycoll where I was born. He moved again soon after to Joppa where I spent most of my childhood. When I was about 11 years old we moved to Grumbla and he worked a smallholding there for the rest of his life. Previously I remember my father had gone out working with Warwick Hosking and his threshing machine, and on the roads trimming hedges.

Later his son Leslie worked with Leonard Hosking and his threshing machine and did farm working.

My older brothers and sisters went into service when they left school; i.e. they lived in on the farms where they were working. Only Jim and I lived at home.

Jim came to our wedding

When I was married in 1940 Jim had just gone away in the Army. On my wedding day he came home. He came to the Chapel but was called out in the middle of the service to go back to his unit. I never even saw him then.

The night that Tregaverah Chapel was bombed we had had word that my brother Jim was missing presumed killed. He had only been away a few weeks. However he had been was taken prisoner.

Thankfully we saw him again after the War was over.

I still walk in to Penzance to do my shopping and ride back. It's uphill ground coming back."

Lewis Grenfell

In Sancreed parish there lived a travelling tailor called Lewis Grenfell. Mr. Weymouth records of him that once seeing a Sedan-chair waiting at the fore door of a big house at Penzance, he slipped into it while the bearers were "off the watch", and tapped the window. At the signal the men took up the chair and carried it to the house of the person who had originally hired it, right at the other end of the town. Directly it was set down, off scampered Lewis, shouting his thanks for the free ride while the chairmen went fuming back again, to meet a scolding from the fare that they had left in the lurch.

Smuggler

Another story is told of journeyman tailor-Lewis Grenfell. One cold mid-winter day, Grenfell and a companion were engaged in removing a cask of brandy from one of the mine adits, which formed a favourite hiding place for smuggled goods in this district. They had just brought out the cask from the tunnel in question when, as luck would have it, an excise man was seen approaching. The tailor's companion, thinking discretion the better part of valour, promptly took to flight and hid himself in a thick furze brake near at hand, leaving the other man to face the situation as best he could.

In answer to the officer's stern inquiries, Grenfell, who appeared to be shaking with the cold, admitted his offence indeed, with the incriminating cask beside him he could do no other but pleaded in extenuation his extreme poverty, the needs of a large family and a sick wife. Finding, however, that pathos produced no effect upon the excise man, the old man begged only that he might be allowed to taste a drop of the precious liquid to warm his shivering bones. To this the officer agreed and handed him a gimlet with which to make a hole in the cask. The tailor's hands were numb however, and his movements so slow that at length the 'sarcher', who was also quite ready for a drink, leapt down from his horse and handing the reins to Grenfell, began 'spiting' the cask himself. Hardly had he begun to do so, when the tailor, perceiving his chance, jumped onto the horse's back and made off at a gallop. The officer thereupon gave chase, and scarcely were both men out of sight round the shoulder of the hill, than the tailor's companion crept out from his hiding place and quickly secured the cask, which, needless to say, the excise man never saw again!

Lewis Grenfell's son, also Lewis, born 1798, farmed at Brane Moor, married twice and had 15 children!

MYRTLE GROVE

Some time after their marriage in 1922 Alfred and Belinda Lawry (nee Hattam) moved from Brane to Myrtle Grove.

Unfortunately tragedy struck the family in 1936 when their only child, Leonard Alfred, died suddenly aged 10 of meningitis.

Belinda Lawry died in 1942 at just 45 years of age, some say of a broken heart. That same year the following advert appeared in the *Cornishman* newspaper:

"TO LET BY TENDER

With vacant Possession at Michaelmas, 1942, or as soon afterwards as may be convenient ALL THAT HOLDING known as "MYRTLE GROVE", in the Parish of Sancreed, in the occupation of Mr Alfred Lawry, who is at present residing at Trannack Mill, Sancreed, who will show applicants over the premises on any morning between 9 and 10.30, or by appointment. Together with TWO FIELDS adjoining, being part of Tregonebris, in the occupation of Mr John Pengelly, the whole amounting to:-

Tillable and homestead 21.025 acres

Crofts .... 10.786 acres

31.811 acres or thereabouts

Tenders to be sent to the undersigned not later than Saturday, 22nd August 1942; the highest of any tender will not necessarily be accepted.
TFB BEAMISH
Chyandour Estate Office, Penzance"
Myrtle Grove was then farmed by a member of the same family when Belinda's niece and her husband, May and Gordon Roberts, moved there.

BOSWARTHAN & ROSE VALLEY

Tommy James, a local farmer and son of William Wearne James formerly of Treganoe. "William and I were born at Boswarthan in the Count House, the big house in the centre. This was the Count House of the old Boswarthan Mine. The valley is full of adits. Further up there are some big shafts.

In 1946, when I was three years old, our family moved down to Rose Valley, a modern house previously occupied by the Bazeleys during the war. Although we lived in the valley we still farmed Boswarthan. In our new home we had bottled gas and every room had gas lights. We thought we were in heaven. At Boswarthan we had had candles and oil lamps but down here it was like going in the Ritz. When we were six, seven or eight William and I would go and play with our only neighbours, John Eddy, William Pengelly and Jesse and Anita Thomas who lived at Tregonebris. This was our domain, a safe environment. Nobody worried about our whereabouts.

I can remember when father would go to Tregonebris to help pull hay or corn on the wagons. These wagons were adapted with drawbars and drawn by tractor. On the back of each wagon were two ropes. We would undo them and they would be like great long snakes. We would lie down, hold the rope and be pulled all round the field. The seats of our trousers would be gone. The way of life was totally different then. Sancreed had a very big Sunday school, as did most villages around, and that's where we attended.

Wilfred Oats was a pig dealer. We kept quite a few pigs and he sold weaners to us. He would suggest a price and Father would say "Too much, take them away again". Wilfred would begin to take them away and then come back again and say, "Have them for so and so". When Father had brought them Wilfred would take out a bit of silver (sixpence) each for William and myself and say, "That's for a bit of luck". We did not get pocket money in those days. Not many children did.

Godfrey Drew's mother died when he was a baby and he came from Sheffield in Paul, when he was about 8 or 9 years old to Boswarthan Bottoms to live with his father. Godfrey took William and I to school on our first day. My brother was 5 and I was 4 years and 8 days old. For the first 2 years we never missed a day and walked in all weather. We were never driven to school. This was quite usual in those days. As far as we were concerned, the car was not meant to take people to school. It was to go to Penzance on a Thursday to take Mother shopping and Father to pick up the *'Cornishman'* newspaper, usually that was the only time the car was used. On odd occasions on a Sunday afternoon the family would be taken out for a drive for an hour or so.

When I left Sancreed School I went to the Grammar School in Penzance. I rode my bike to Tregonebris and caught the bus with William Pengelly.

We were renting Boswarthan. Father had the opportunity to buy Little Sellan and so we moved on to land that we owned but still rented Boswarthan. Later in life we had the opportunity to buy that farm too."

LITTLE BOSWARTHAN

Marriage

Richard Norman Hosking (Norman): I got married to Kathleen Trezise at the age of twenty five at Sancreed Church, the Rev John Stona officiating at 9.00 in the morning. The teacher of Sancreed School (who taught both of us for a time) brought the children across to see us come out of church. It was during the 2nd World War and a cottage at Trerice Bridge was empty.

Kathleen, my wife, her sister and parents moved there from Penzance after being frightened by the bombs before moving to Skimmel Bridge. So we went to Skimmel Bridge for the wedding breakfast before going off on honeymoon by train to Plymouth. The honeymoon was supplied free of charge by my in-law's friends – Mr and Mrs Loten.

This was my first holiday since leaving school. Plymouth at this time was mainly heaps of rubble. Buses and cars had to be driven with only dipped headlights. Mr Loten was most particular to blackout the window because of the danger of any light being visible to enemy aircraft. Their house of course had modern sanitation, which I experienced for the first time!

We walked around the city including Mutley Plain which was a part not so badly damaged by the bombs and fires. A week was soon gone and it was back to work. We came home to our house at Sellan to two chairs, a table and a bed, which my mother had brought second hand.

January 1st 1956.

The great day arrived. We were moving from Sellan where I had lived for thirty five years to Little Boswartnan, about two miles away. The tenancy commenced on September 30 1955 but since work had to be done to the premises, moving in was delayed. During those three months my brothers and I went to Boswarthan to help the estate workers with the alterations. The Cornish slab was taken out and replaced with a Rayburn. All the rooms in the house needed some work; even the outside toilet was repaired. In the yard the cowshed was modernised, a dairy put up, barn, yearling house, calves houses all repaired."

Kathleen: "Norman used to have to go over Sellan and work so that they would come back and help him and we could borrow the tractor from them. It was a very busy life. I kept poultry – ducks, turkeys and hens and we sold the eggs to the egg man who collected them once a week.

It was three months before we bought a car and then we were able to go and do some shopping, although most of it could be done through the butcher and the grocer's vans coming around.

We had four children born at Sellan, Alan, Vivienne, Malcolm and Marilyn. At Boswarthan we had Simon, and 10½ years later, Jonathan."

Their son Alan: "Our water came from a well outside the back door, pumped by hand. There was also a windmill at Gold Herring, which pumped water to the farm, but in the summer both were often dry. We then used to put a tank on the trailer and travel to Trerice bridge where father would pass buckets (filled from the well there) up to me to tip into the tank. We would make this trip several times in a week as the cattle made short work of each tankful. On occasions it was bought from & delivered by the fire brigade.

We had little in the way of farm machinery...this was borrowed from father's brothers at Sellan. I can remember driving the tractor on a moonlit evening whilst father off loaded limestone from the trailer to be spread over the field."

Television upside down

Kathleen: "One November morning after most of the family had gone out and the men were out milking, there was a sudden great flash of lightening and the lights went out then came back on again.

I went back indoors and looked around. Everything looked alright except the plug into the back of the wireless was blown off.

In the other room the television was upside down and on fire and the telephone split to bits. Lucky I was outside at the time it happened. I knew if I shouted to the men they wouldn't hear me. I thought if I ran out to them the house could be on fire. Knowing the television was not plugged in I got a bucket of water and threw over it. The lightening had come in on the telephone wires. One of our chairs was burnt and the dog was frightened out of its life. Then Norman and Simon came in, having no idea what had happened inside. They wondered what I was doing with the smoke coming out! Three new telephone poles had to be erected and all the burnt wires replaced."

October 22nd 1984

Norman: "Today it is dull and dark with thick misty rain, wind blowing and not very warm so it is difficult to imagine the hot dry summer of eighty-four. The rain of the last month has made no difference to the height of water in Drift Dam. The drought started at the end of March. Hay and silage crops were light but we had to start feeding them to the livestock in September because of the shortage of grass. This looks as though it will be a long and expensive winter for the dairymen of the southwest.

Our swallows hatched three lots of young, firstly four and then five and finally three which flew away on the sixteenth of October. Maybe there will not be another year like '84 for a long time. The last dry summer was in '76.

Last evening a communion service was held at Sancreed Church. There were two baptisms and twelve confirmations by the Bishop of St Germans, the church was full and after the service there was tea."

Once or twice in his last few months of life, Norman spoke of the fact that he had had everything he wanted in life – his wife, their children and his farm.

CARN EUNY and other ancient sites

Carn Euny is a well-cared-for Iron Age Village. The houses with their rooms and hearths are easy to see, as is the fogou and the stone-covered drains.

Fogous have been variously interpreted as hiding places, cold storage for food, or religious ritual structures.

The most beautiful of these underground constructions is at Carn Euny, on the south western slope of a hill on which stands the fort of Caer Barn, in Sancreed parish. Perhaps you will only discover it when you find that you have walked onto the top of the domed chamber and that you

Fogue passageway.

are looking down into a mysterious walled cavity beneath your feet. The chamber is approached by a narrow entrance which branches off from the north end of the corridor; it is about 14 feet in diameter.

The gallery itself is some 42 feet long, roofed by great slabs of granite laid across it. Copeland Borlase discovered some coarse red and black pottery here, together with a piece of smooth red glaze, which he took for Samian ware.

Dr Vernon of Penberth, with others, was excavating at the Carn Euny ancient site in 1927/28.

Excavations at **Carn Euny** have shown Neothlithic activities; also that it has been continuously inhabited from around 300BC until the late Roman period in the 4th Century AD. A peaceful, walled site, high on the hill above Brane, it has a significant vantage point over the surrounding area. It shows different types of dwellings due to its development over a long period of habitation whilst there is the remains of an unfinished Iron Age Fort at **Caer Bran**, enclosing a Bronze Age cairn.

Discovered by W C Borlase in 1863, **Brane Barrow** is purported to be one of the smallest entrance graves in Cornwall and is thought to date from C2500BC. As it provided shelter for local farm animals, it had not been robbed of its stones!

The Holywell is possibly pre-Christian. Situated below Carn Euny, healing ceremonies were carried out here well into the 18th century. At the end of the 19th century, the Misses Quiller-Couch were recorded to have stated that sickly children were brought (from miles around) to be cured, especially on the first three Wednesdays in May. We no longer know why these three days were significant. Children were washed in the well and it once had a great reputation for healing.

CHAPTER 5

GRUMBLA AREA

SANCREED BEACON The Beacon 172m above sea level rises above the village. It affords extensive views across to Mounts Bay and around. This granite upland, now owned by The Cornwall Heritage Trust, was probably inhabited during the Bronze Age. Remains of two burial mounds can be seen on the summit and the remains of what is believed to be a Bronze Age hut stands on the western slope. Sancreed Beacon also boasts evidence of prehistoric field boundaries. Open workings and old shafts provide evidence of tin mining there in the mid 19th century - Wheal Argus, was also known as Beacon Mine. This Beacon would have been one of a series that were set alight as a warning of imminent invasion during the Napoleonic wars.

Suspicious Aircraft

Ken Wood former policeman "As a young Constable in the early 1970's, and having been given the area west of Penzance to patrol, I very soon assessed the Parish of Sancreed to be one of quiet harmony for most of the time. The inhabitants were mostly friendly and often gave useful information regarding odd happenings.

One such offering was noted as, ' An aircraft making nocturnal visits to land just behind Sancreed Beacon'. This resulted in my given the task to patrol the area with a view to identifying the plane and taking the necessary steps to evaluate the reason. At this time there had been various cases of landings by suspected illegal immigrants, and also of smuggling contraband - an aircraft had never been used for this type of event in West Cornwall before, but there was always the chance of a 'first' The Irish Terrorist movement at the time gave rise to various thoughts of security of explosives stores at mines and other storage points. An airborne raid was, perhaps, a possibility.

Several nights of keeping observation in the area resulted in no sightings of aircraft - nor much else with movement!

After giving several negative reports on the subject, having discreetly enquired at Lands End Airport if such landings had been noticed (without positive result), the subject was placed 'for casual observations when in the area'.

Whilst on the night shift, it was also necessary to visit various secure establishments during the patrol. One of these was the Land's End Radio Station at St.Just, and it was during a 4.00am visit one night to make contact with the Duty Radio Operator, that I chanced to mention the suspicious aircraft landing at Sancreed. "Oh, that was probably me", said the fellow, quite nonchalantly. "I used to bring my old Auster Aircraft in to see some friends who lived near the Beacon. The Auster was capable of taking off, and landing, in a short distance (about 50 yards), and I could quite easily drop it in on the old Golf Links there". I made no disclosure of how close he came to being surrounded and apprehended as a suspected gunrunner. But I learnt a lot about the adaptability of an Auster."

'Dream Princess', by Elizabeth Forbes, featuring Johnny Richards of Drift, see pages 39/40. Painting by permission of the Trustees of the Royal Institution of Cornwall.

Sheila Hicks (nee Warren).
Spent her childhood at Lesbew.
See pages 56/57 for the full story.

Sancreed School 1980.
(Full caption with list of names is
featured on page 20).

Flying tractor page 54. Where the tractor finally came to rest, viewed by onlookers from the road above. Inset: Eamonn today.

Chycoll see pages 92/93.

Margo Maeckelberghe and one of her paintings at her exhibition at the St Ives Tate, 2008.

Below: Tregannick House, featured in Chapter 5.

*School Certificate of Merit, for Proficiency in
Religious Knowledge.
Awarded to Mary Hattam 1916.
Mary Hattam and family are featured in Chapter 6.*

*Terry Shorland
at 'feeding time'.*

Below: The Famous Drift Swans see pages 35/36.

The sign for the prestigious Penzance Golf Club, Golf Links, at Sellan Sancreed has been carefully saved by Margaret German daughter of, and James Osborne grandson of, Sancreed's most famous golfer Cyril Lane, see page 143.

Picture detail clearly shows where the original Golf Links words were painted over.

Below: 'Ponies at Ennestreven' painting by Sarah Carter.

Roskennals Mill, page 127.

ENNESTREVEN

Edith Try 99 years old

"We saw Marconi walking down the street in Causewayhead with Betty Paynter. We all dashed out of the shops to see them. I was a young girl then; aged 16 at the time. (In 1924 Edith worked at Bridgers the bookshop, which at that time was in Causewayhead).

I was brought up at Grumbla then Ennestreven Farm. Yes, I was able to milk the cows but I did not like pig-killing day. The pigs were screeching. Having chicken for dinner was a luxury in those days. I remember having bread milk and sugar in a basin. You got used to it, we wouldn't think of it now. Rabbits were a source of income and a leg of rabbit we adored. Father trapped them.

I was an only child. My brother died in infancy.

Lands End Honeymoon

Mother was married in 1908, and where did they spend their honeymoon? At Lands End for the day! She dressed beautifully and wore ostrich feathers - her father was out in Africa mining, earning the money. We used to sleep on tiger skin rugs!

I took my husband Oliver up to see Gran at Carnyorth when she had given up the farm He couldn't believe he was sleeping under these tiger skin rugs.

I remember going up Beacon Hill when the First War ended. I couldn't walk. Father had to put me over his shoulders. We went up to the top of the Beacon to see what was going on, like the fireworks going off from the boats in the bay. One day we were chatting to Lord Falmouth, a friend of my uncle. He said, "You know Edie, there's no place like Beacon Hill!"

I remember Sancreed School and Mr Martin and Miss Reynolds who taught us. I used to have the cane. I think Sancreed School was a nice school. I was there until I was 10 then I went to the County School. I am now the oldest surviving girl from those days.

We used to go to Trevarthan Chapel and in the summer we went on Sunday school outings to Carbis Bay. We rode on wagons pulled by horses.

On the end of the chapel there was Ellis' blacksmiths shop. My father and other men used to go there in the evening and sit around and chat. A similar shack there was a carpenter's shop. It was owned by someone called Oats but not a relative of ours.

We used to visit the butcher in Penzance in our pony and jingle. At weekends we visited my grandfather Richard Oates of Jericho. He would insist that his family were all round him. He had 12 children and was left a widower when his youngest son Athelston was only 12 months old. He would offer a home to Doctor Barnardo boys. A very good man and real religious 'Bless the Lord' and all that kind of thing. A Barnardo boy named Arnold married his daughter and they went to America and made good.

In Sancreed we would have whist drives, and activities at both the chapel and church. Rev Stona, the vicar, was good to the whole community. We all paid our tithes to him. Sancreed feast is at Whitsun but we kept St Just Feast as our main event. We used to look after the boys and walk up and down. There was a good crowd of young people, the Rogers' all had children, the Hoskens in Bosence, the Hattams in Botrea, and the Semmens were in Trannack. Janet Semmens and I went to the County School together.

I used to enjoy visiting Nelly Hicks' at the large house called Treganoe. It was a lovely place.

I took over playing the organ from Martin Oats at Sancreed Chapel. I remember him taking his basket around the farms collecting eggs and being congratulated on the way I played. Mrs Oats seemed like old Queen Mary to me. You had to be 'just so' with her.

We knew the Lanes very well. They lived and worked on the Golf Links and had a son called Cyril. I used to try to play golf with him. It was not really golf. We were just kids. I was often up there for teas.

My father died at 37 and mother and I went to Carnyorth to the house next to my grandmother to live. We didn't like it there. The Armstrongs offered to have us stay at Nansalverne.

Later Mother bought 2 Weeths Cottages in Penzance and we went there to live. She lived there for the rest of her life and I was married from there. I met my husband when we were children. We had three offspring, two girls and a boy. They all went to college. My daughter Margo Maeckelberghe is an artist. She painted mainly scenes from Cornwall. Her pictures are being shown all over the world. She was friendly with Betty Paynter who sometimes came to tea.

In the *Cornishman* of Jan. 12th 1985, "Sixty year wedding well worth a Try. A well known Penzance couple have just celebrated 65 years of marriage. Oliver and Evie Try met as teenagers and were married at St John's Church Penzance. The youthful looking couple have enjoyed a quiet Christmas with their family". My husband and I had 68 years together.

Von Ribbentrop

In the mornings, before the War, JoachimVon Ribbentrop used to regularly come horse riding around our farm with Carmyn, Leslie Oats' wife. He was staying with the Oats' at the big house, Tregannick. Ribbentrop did go round the farm!"

Lord St Levan: *"Before the Second World War, Hitler's Foreign Minister Joachim Von Ribbentrop was the German Ambassador in England. He used to stay in a Hotel in St Ives during the summer holidays. On one occasion he was invited to lunch at a country house in West Cornwall, and was passing St Michaels' Mount on his way. After the war, the chauffeur disclosed this conversation to a local newspaper, which unfortunately, I have lost. According to the chauffeur, he was called on to serve in the army during the war. By coincidence he was one of the*

Joahim von Ribbentrop and right with Hitler.

guards in the prison at Nuremburg where the leading Nazis were held for war crimes after the German defeat.

This chauffer asked permission to talk to von Ribbentrop after he had been sentenced to death, as he wanted to remind him about the conversation he had once heard. Permission was given a fortnight before Von Ribbentrop was due to be hanged. Ribbentrop's only reply was "Things are very different now". I had often heard this story when staying at St Michael's Mount after the War. I do not know if there were any other sources for the story apart from the account of the chauffeur in the newspaper interview".

Dr. Eric Richards: *"Von Ribbentrop came to Cornwall before the War and was entertained at Trengwainton by Colonal Edward Bolitho who was then Lord Lieutenant of Cornwall and therefore whose duty it was to entertain Royalty and representatives of foreign nations. So it was his duty to entertain von Ribbentrop who was German Foreign Minister. Some in Cornwall thought Col Bolitho had Nazi sympathies which was not the case".*

From another source: **"An occasional visitor to Trengwainton House in pre-WWII years was the then German Foreign Minister, Joachim Von Ribbentrop, who, it is said, travelled in a light aircraft - landing on an unofficial airstrip west of Penzance".**

Tregenna Castle brochure: *"Tregenna Castle has played host to many prominent visitors. One notable person was Herr von Ribbentrop, the German Ambassador to Great Britain before the Second World War. It was a widely held belief that St Ives would never be bombed, because Hitler had promised Tregenna to von Ribbentrop as a personal residence after Germany had conquered Great Britain".*

Ribbentrop was Hitler's German ambassador to Britain in 1937 and tried to negotiate a friendship pact with Britain. He went around this country hoping to influence people in authority. This included visits to West Cornwall.

He made lots of visits 1933 to 1939 to Britain, France, Italy and the USA. He was very pro-Western but unpopular with governments who resented his superior and bullying manner. He even did the Hitler salute when being presented to the Queen at the Court of St James. The full story of von Ribbentrop's visits to West Cornwall 70 years ago may never be told.

Secret Love

It appears that Ribbentrop's aide had a liaison with a local young lady at this time, 1937.

In the spring of 1939 she visited Berlin and was a guest at the British Embassy of a friend, another young lady, who was at that time also staying there. There was also the legend of a silent plane landing in this area at Christmas 1940.

Hitler's Foreign Minister, one of Germany's most notorious war criminals, Joachim von Ribbentrop was, in 1946, found guilty and executed during the Nuremburg War Crimes Trial.

Margo Maeckelberghe

"My mother EdithTry nee Oats met my father Oliver Try when they were both at the Grammar School. They had two daughters and 10 years later David was born. Her parents had owned Ennestreven and later passed it on to her. When David was old enough she passed it on to him.

I had a great affection for Sancreed and painted it in a different way from anybody else.

I used to know John Miller very well. We were both painters and liked each other's work!"

Margo studied at the Penzance School of Art and at the Bath Academy of Art. She worked with such artists as Bryan Wynter and Peter Lanyon, later exhibiting with such artists as John Miller, Jack Pender, Derek Guthrie and Alan Lowndes.

When asked in an interview with Michael Williams why she thought artists were drawn to Cornwall, Margo stated, "I've thought about this a lot. This crystal clear light, I think, is the explanation. Then of course there's this timeless quality about Cornwall."

Recently Margo held an exhibition of her paintings at the Tate Gallery with a record number of viewers.

David Try: Ennestreven started to be cleared in 1648. It had been moorland. From Clive Carter I learned there were Alms Houses here. Granddad, (Richard Oats of Jericho), bought it from Lord Falmouth and Scoble Armstrong.

Martin and his son Leslie Oats

Martin Oats, a small farmer, son of a St Just miner, started a new career by going around the farms with a basket collecting eggs. Later he used a pony and trap.

Sometime before 1897 he set himself up as egg and butter merchant at Grumbla. The 1901 census showed he was 41 years old and born at St Just, as was his wife Jane, nee Hocking, who was 40. Their sons Fred aged 11 and Leslie aged 2 were both born at Sancreed.

Leslie Oates with coach and pair.

By 1914 Martin's business had much expanded. Kellys Directory described him as 'Martin Oats butter & egg merchant; agent for cream separators & dairy utensils of every.

About 1925 the description in Kelly's was 'M.Oats & Son creamery proprietors & merchants'. The creamery (dairy) was at Lower Grumbla, across the road from his original premises. When Martin moved into Trewithen Road, Penzance,

Leslie Oats took over the business. Around this time Leslie's first wife Priscilla died and he married Carmynowe (known as Carmyn).

In 1932, Gladys Gendall nee Remphrey, now 91 years old, worked at the dairy, packing cream in huge tins to send away. For a few weeks in the summer, at Christmas and Easter she worked from 8 in the morning to 11 at night. Then Carmyn Oats and her housekeeper Ann Jenkin would come and take over packing cream throughout the night.

Ann Jenkin was brought up in a cottage next door to Joan Berryman. Her father was blind. When she left school she came to live with the Oats family.

TREGANNICK

Leslie Oats

When Leslie Oats first married he lived in a bungalow down by the dairy. By 1935 the dairy was renamed Primrose Dairy.

Around 1936 he had Tregannick a fine Bavarian German type house built, designed by the architect Geoffrey Bazeley. Upstairs there was an overhang where a person could sleep under cover outdoors. His first wife had contracted tuberculosis.

Everything inside the house was 'modernist', oak panelled and the furniture bought from Heals in London.

At one time someone scrawled on the roof with tar "Bonus Villa" when there had been a difference of opinion with the farmers over a Christmas bonus.

In 1937 Von Ribbentrop the German ambassador stayed with the Oats' at Tregannick and went horse riding each morning with Carmyn. He apparently promised them that Primrose Dairy would never be bombed!

David Try: "Under what is now the modernised kitchen there is an air raid shelter in Tregannick. They have put a new cover over it, but it is still there".

Tregannick House.

Bolventer Harriers and Western Hunt

Leslie Oats kept a small pack of harriers that he had started at Bolventor and kept them there throughout the 2nd world war. During that conflict he looked after the hounds belonging to the Western Hunt. After the war the hounds went back to the kennels, and he brought the Harriers back to Sancreed where he hunted them. They were kept at Grumbla in the winter and at Trannack Mill in the summer.

Alfred Olds: "Leslie Oats had horses and he had hackney carriages. His were really top class horses, which he showed everywhere – even in London. He kept about twenty hackney carriages until he thought he was getting on in life when he started selling them off. He didn't want them to be in a sale after he died. He really knew about horses and looking over one he wouldn't miss much.

Ann Jenkin lived with the Oats family from the time she left school until the time she died. She was a wonderful kind woman. She and Mrs Oats used to come to Church quite often".

Leslie Oats died at Tregannick in 1992 aged 93. His wife Carmyn died in 1998.

Fred Oats

Fred Oats, Leslie's older brother was born about 1890 and trained as a Rolls Royce engineer.

Bob Rogers: "Fred became a racing driver and car salesman. Before the war he raced cars at Goodwood, and when he lived in London used to sell second hand cars from a showroom near Tottenham Court Rd.

When in Cornwall, he lived with his father Martin Oats at 'Venton Vean', Trewithen Road, Penzance, where he continued to live after his father died.

I bought a Jaguar car from Fred just after the war. He was selling cars out of Barclay and Jose's, Trafalgar Garage in Morrab Road.

Dr Dyke: "Fred had OM Italian cars. He raced them at Goodwood. Both Fred and Leslie used to race boats at Mounts Bay and Hayle. I had one of Fred's racing boats here for a while. It was quite slick.

Catchall Dairy Grumbla

From about 1925 to 1938 there were two dairies at Sancreed: Catchall at Catchall and Primrose Dairy at Grumbla.

Having moved to St Erth in 1938, Primrose Dairy sold their Sancreed premises at Lower Grumbla to Catchall Dairy. In 1939 they became the largest employer in Sancreed.

In 1942 when Bottoms Milk Factory closed at St Levan, that milk was brought to Catchall Dairy. The good will and fixed assets of Catchall Dairy were sold in 1943 to Cow and Gate, who later became Unigate.

The Dairy at Grumbla carried on until 1962 when it ceased trading and all the milk from West Cornwall was taken direct to St Erth.

Early milk factory vans.

EMPLOYEES' TALES

Romance at Catchall Dairy   Jack and Alice Branwell

Jack Branwell: "I started working at the factory in 1943 when I was 14. I did all sorts of jobs there, from making butter boxes, tipping the milk, to doing night shifts in the milk powder room. A girl called Alice worked in the laboratory with Mr Gregory, where they tested the milk.

Desmond Wearne whom I worked with was going with a girl from Botallack. It was coming up for Corpus Christi Fair, so he asked me if I was going. I bucked up enough courage and asked Alice if she would come with me. We went up to the fair and after that started going out together. In 1947 I was called up for National Service and went in the Royal Air Force for two years. We were married in March 1950 and have been together ever since.

Primrose Dairy, later Catchall.

After the war I went back to work at the dairy and stayed there until the dairy shut down. Then I went back into the RAF again. I went to the Persian Gulf for a year and came back with a lovely suntan. Someone from St Just saw Alice and me in Penzance and went back to St Just, up to my sister's house to tell her "I have just seen Jack's wife walking around Penzance with a black man." We had to go up the next day to explain that I was that black man!

All the farmers in West Penwith had their milk collected by lorry and brought to the dairy. Most of the milk was sent up country; it was taken by road tanker to Penzance railway station, pumped into rail tankers and taken 'up the line'. Geoff Hardiman was the tanker driver. He made several trips each day. Some milk was used to make butter in a large revolving vat. Fred Gendall was the main butter maker. Some milk was used to make clotted cream. In charge of this operation was Jimmy Olds.

The separated 'skimmed milk' was piped down to the powder room, where it was passed over huge heated rollers and turned into dried milk. This was bagged up or put in tins. Some went to make Cow and Gate baby food.

Working at Catchall dairy were the best working years of my life. I worked there for nearly 20 years. They were the biggest employers in the area then. I could earn more than my father did underground working at Geevor mine.

Levant mine disaster

Talking of my father, he was in the Levant disaster 1919 and was saved by my grandfather lying on top of him. Sadly, my grandfather was killed. Father (who was 19 at the time) was brought up for dead with head injuries. He recovered and went to America to stay with his brother to recuperate. He worked there in a car factory. My sister and I were born there.

At Catchall dairy we used to have socials and Christmas parties. A van took people home afterwards. Workers came from all around the area. I used to cycle to work with

Jim Eddy from St Just. One day after work, Jim said lets see how fast we can get to St Just. We did it in just under 15 minutes. It nearly killed me! On another occasion I cycled to the dairy one morning when it was snowing. I worked all day and tried to cycle home. When I got to the wireless station at St Just, I had to get off and push the bike. The snow was that deep that I could feel that I was walking on top of cars which were buried under the snow!"

Bronte connection?

John Bremble had 8 children all baptised at Sancreed between 1605 and 1630: John, Margaret, Martyn, Ann, Richard, Walter, Jane and Edward.

It is possible that Jack Branwell and the Penzance Branwell's, ancestors of the famous Bronte sisters, are descended from this same John Bremble.

Trevor Richards

"I used to attend Sancreed Chapel Sunday school and as well as the annual charabanc trip to Carbis Bay beach we also had sports and games on Jim Stevens' field, which was next to the chapel. After the sports we would adjourn to the schoolroom for tea and saffron buns.

As time went on, Father, who was driving a milk lorry, collecting milk from the farms into Catchall Dairy, Grumbla, was taken ill. I had to leave my job and drive the milk lorry for about 12 months. When father was well enough to drive again I managed to get a job at the dairy. Well, I did numerous jobs there. I helped Fred Gendall to make butter, and I was up on the 'stand' tipping the milk out of the churns as they came off the milk lorries.

Good deed repaid by a warning!

Although earning quite good money, one of the workers, Garfield, was not allowed 'pocket money' by his wife. To help him out, I used to alter his pay packet by 2/6 or 5/- so his wife wouldn't realise he was having a bit of pocket money from his wages. This worker had a little cows house and he dug a stone out from the inside wall to store his money there. As time went on, his wife got a bit suspicious about how he could afford cigarettes and followed him out to the cows' house one evening. His secret was out and I got into trouble and had a 'warning' from my boss!

A Ghost

At Catchall dairy, some of the milk was tipped and separated, then piped into a massive holding tank, where it was then fed through huge heated rollers, which turned the separated milk into solid sheets. The dried milk would then pass down chutes into the powder room, where it was bagged and laced up ready for dispatch. Again on one night shift I was working there I thought I would pay the chap working in the powder room a visit. I went up and got one of Dora's white coats from the kitchen, where we made the tea and crept down to the powder room and got up on top of the bags of powdered milk and I waved my arms around, making ghostly noises, because they had been saying that there was a ghost down there. I saw this chap looking around to see where the noises were coming from. When he saw me, he said, "There is a ghost down here," and he took off up the stairs and we couldn't get him back there for the rest of the night!

You Sancreed boys make me sick!

I was friendly with Andrew Armour from Grumbla. He used to borrow his father's car for outings all over West Cornwall. Late at night returning home, in order that Andrew's father had enough petrol to get to work next day, we would knock on Brenda Rowe's door. She ran a garage at Buryas Bridge and would poke her head out of the window asking, "Is that you Sancreed boys again, what do you want?" We replied, "Petrol" upon which she would come down in her dressing gown, walk the 100 yards to the garage and would not be best pleased to learn she had been dragged out of bed again for half a gallon of petrol! She used to say, "You Sancreed boys make me sick".

Mick Angwin

"I went in the old milk factory here one day and the old brass valve hanging in the corner had been cut. Next day I went in and it had been cut again. I went in every morning for a week and I could see that Brass valve had been cut a little more. I went in one morning and I thought, "They will be through that tonight. So that night I put 2 guard dogs in there to protect the property. The next morning I went in and couldn't believe my eyes. There was a man sitting in the corner very upset. The dogs would not let him out. That brass valve was there for years afterwards.

In 1971/2 I owned some lorries and I was working on a shoestring, I had one lorry parked up for a week and Leslie Oats asked, "Why is that lorry parked there?" I said, "It needs a new engine". He said, "Well put one in". I said, "I haven't got the money to do it". He came back with a cheque. Six months later I went across the road to give it back to him and he said to me, "Didn't ask for that did I?" He didn't want to know.

(Mick had been kind to him and his wife when she was in hospital.)

Joan Berryman

Mick Angwin: "When Joan's place caught fire she went in hospital with smoke inhalation. Afterward they were going to put her down to Helston for a short stay. We couldn't let them do that because Joan belongs up here. So she came to stay with us for 3 or 4 weeks. She wouldn't do anything on a Sunday - not even her knitting.

Her mother died in 1939 when she was quite young after which she cared for her father, Arthur Berryman.

Arthur had a pet pig that sometimes came in the house. Arthur would rest his feet on the pig by the Rayburn. One day Arthur had collapsed and when they tried to get to him the pig was lying against the door.

Joan worked for Brian Warren for a while in the café and restaurant on the Terrace, Penzance."

Contrary to popular belief, pigs are actually very clean animals which is why they are sometimes kept as pets.

JOAN BERRYMAN'S RECORDING

"We went to school when we were five, we left when we were fourteen. The two subjects I didn't like were History and Geography.

My sister died when she was three and I being the only one there, I was sort of spoilt. She had fair hair and blue eyes and was the pretty one. She was only ill a few days and then she died and I asked my mother, if I could have another baby sister? I never had another baby sister.

I never had a boyfriend. I met some very nice men and that's it, but my head ruled my heart. Father said that men wouldn't ask me out because they would expect that I would expect them to work as hard as I do!

I didn't have a young life, just hard work all my life, and now I'm in retirement. And I'm enjoying it.

I taught myself to knit as I've gone on; it started at school, perhaps jumpers or cardigans. I like doing an Arran pattern. I like making my own jumpers but I never have time for that because someone is always having a baby and then I got to knit for them.

Bygone years

Years ago you married the boy next door - it was easy - but now people have moved away and strangers have come along. It was quite a community here fifty years ago - we had a blacksmith's shop just up the top of the road, a carpenter's shop just a bit further down and we had a school and two Chapels, and one of the finest local cricket teams. 'Course we had no water and no electricity, that's all come since the war. We used to catch all the rainwater we could during the winter, it didn't last us through the summer. The Chapel's gone, the school's gone, there's nothing left now.

I almost went to pieces when my mother died. Mother just collapsed and died and that was it. I called father in and she was talking to me, we all had breakfast together and I thought she had fallen over or something, but she was dead. The Doctor came, the Nurse came, and people came. She died; it was just like blowing out a candle. Then six months after my mother died my father had a stroke so I had to look after him then, and I've looked after this place ever since. That's something you never really get over. Just learn to live with it.

The cattle are a bit fat. I'm trying to get them thinner and then I can get them in calf. I drink a lot of milk and I think that's maybe why I keep going. I was given a calf once which was born three weeks ahead of time and I gave her a lot of milk, three times a day, and she stayed here. What I planned to do was feed her up and to put her to market but she changed her mind and when she came into season she jumped the field and found a bull and got herself in calf so she's been here ever since and she's about fifteen years old now.

Joan Berryman.

If anybody's got something they don't want "Take it up to Joan, she'll do with it".

People think all they got to do is just ring up-she'll have a chicken, a few eggs, just ring up.

Come out on top

Things have to be done every day, no matter what the weather is, I can't just say, 'I won't do it today'. The animals have to be looked after every day. Life is hard sometimes. I overcome the difficulties and carry on. I have my pension, the pigs are gone. It makes a difference now with my pension each week.

1 don't have a day off. Thursday mornings 1 go to Penzance to collect my pension and do my shopping. My days off are very rare. I go in the Bank, up in the lift and put the eggs in the room there, pick up any empty cartons been left for me and out through the back door.

Get myself pasties to bring home, get my papers and then I go the Co-op to get my groceries, then 1 come home.

There's always something to do, people to see, people to talk to. Fridays a man comes with feed for the animals. I have customers. It's a hive of industry really. I've been here seventy-two years. It's a long time in one place. Thank God he never gives us what we can't bear or endure. I've had enough anyway. I'm not deeply religious but I'm sure there's a God or something up there or somewhere. He got me through very difficult times and I've come out on top and I'm still here."

Joan had a good sense of humour. The lorry driver came with pellets for the chicken.

"Some cold out today Joan. I hope you've got your mistletoe ready for Christmas".

"Nobody's given me a kiss under the mistletoe yet Keith", said Joan laughing "I don't think they will start now." "Oh, you never know", he said.

Growing up at Sancreed.

Penny Thomas nee Adams: The moors used to be our playground. We used to open our back doors, climb over the fence and play up on the moors. We used to watch foxes up on the moor playing with their cubs. The old pig farm up there used to be our hut.

We used to shoot rabbits and bring them home and mum skinned them and we had rabbit stew quite often. All of us went lamping. The girls held the lamps and the brothers used to shoot the rabbits. Dad worked a lot; money was really tight in those days. Lamping and shooting was a way of life.

We did not have television for years. We made our own entertainment. We used to go down Skimmel woods, scrumping apples.

Hugh Rowe used to teach at Sunday school and arrange the Sunday school outings with the great tea buns.   Jethro used to come up our place quite often and have tea up there. We used to call him Jeff. That's where he got his name from – Jeff Rowe then Jethro.

Billie and Richard Adams, Jethro, Michael Adams.

When we were up Grumbla we had no electricity and no water so we used to have to go up and fetch water. Bathing was in a tin bath on the floor once a week – the dirtiest one used to get in last! Cleanest in first! I think it was good living up Green Lane.

Luxury

I used to think it was a luxury to get an orange, a bar of chocolate and a pair of socks or something like that for Christmas. If you wanted to buy something you used to have to get a job or do things around the house to earn your pocket money or do something for the neighbours. We worked for them all. We used to go down and help put flags out for the gymkhana in the field behind Sanceed Chapel for pocket money. The institute had an old wood floor and we used to save up the tea leaves in a bucket and sprinkle them on the floor, then brush them up to stop the dust from rising.

Trixie Rowe was a lovely lady who sometimes after Church used to invite us in and give us a cup of tea, milk or lemonade with special buns she had made.

CHYCOLL

The Will of William Hosking, Yeoman   Dated 25th May 1745

This will was made by a man who was born some three hundred years ago, and whose family farmed at Brane. Described as a yeoman meant that he owned some freehold property and was in a fair way of going on since he left his daughter £100, either for a dowry or to enable her to be able to pay her way in the world if she did not marry, and not to be described as a pauper.

The fact that he left his wife the bed and bedding was a term to mean that she was to be part of the household and to have her living as long as she lived.

It would appear that his sister Jane Tonkin (nee Hosken) was in some danger of becoming a widow - a sick husband perhaps who was less well-off, and so he makes sure that she had a roof over her head. Chycoll still stands, so Jane must have heeded the warning and kept it in repair.

William Hosken's bequests:

1. *Unto Catherine my wife the bed and bedding.*
2. *To my daughter Jane £100 (she was unmarried).*
3. *To my sister Jane Tonkin the house in Chycowl in case she is left a widow and to keep it in repair.*
4. *Ten shillings to the poor of Sancreed.*
5. *The residue to my son John Hosken and appoint him executor.*

William signed his will with a good hand and it was witnessed by James Hosken, John Hosken and Martin Wallis.

The latter was the same man who entertained John Wesley at Tredinney where he had two farms, and who also lived at Brane for some time.

We can only surmise, but it appears as though William Hosken was not an elderly man, since there are no grandchildren mentioned in the will.

A brief history of the property known now as 'Chycoll' – formerly 'Chycolls' and 'Chycoles' – David Ceredig-Evans

In the parish of Sancreed, on his own freehold of Lower Drift, lived Peter Harvey; his youngest child Elizabeth (whose baptism was, like one or two other cases, accidentally omitted from the register) married Martin Rowe, of Brahau and Chycolls, Sancreed, in 1798.

1827 Sancreed baptismal register, 29th December 1827 John Rowe was baptised. His parents were Martin (labourer) and Elizabeth Rowe of Chycoles.

In August 1858, Edward Jenkin married Elizabeth Warren of St Buryan. Then in the **1861** census, Elizabeth Warren is shown as living at Chycolls.

1925 August, Charles Jefferys, a farmer of Chycoll, sold the dwelling house, garden and premises at Chycoll to Miss Mary Jane Bosence.

1942 On September 25th/26th, a bomb from an enemy aircraft almost totally destroyed the offices of Arthur William Hext Harvey, solicitor at 6 North Parade, Penzance. In this building was the personal deed box of Arthur Harvey and contained within were the documents relating to Chycoll, which were all destroyed.

1867 March, Mary Jane Bosence's brother, Robert Bosence, sold Chycoll to Gordon Shaw. Electricity was connected during this year.

1984 September, Mabel Shaw sold Chycoll to Mr and Mrs Carter.

1995 September, David & Coralie Ceredig-Evans brought Chycoll from Irene Manhire and Bernard Carter and now live at the property with their three children.

ENNIS

The Grenfells
George Grenfell maps out the Congo

A distinguished son of Cornwall was George Grenfell, Baptist missionary and explorer who carried out a hydrographic survey of the Congo that added valuable scientific knowledge of the interior of Africa

George Grenfell won the respect of the Admiralty by designing a special twin-screw steamer, the famous PEACE. Having planned it, he arranged for it to be built on prefabricated lines. Three relays of natives carried the eight hundred component parts overland to Stanley Pool, and there, (the two engineers having died of fever), he put the parts together with the aid of eight natives.

Whilst on his voyages, hippopotami left their teeth marks on the steel plates of the

Plaque unveilling of George Grenfell.

Peace; poisoned arrows dropped quivering to the deck; an enemy tribe attacked in 50 canoes-but Grenfell sailed on, charting the Congo and its tributaries on a scale of one inch to a mile. When he ran short of engine oil he used his last tin of butter, and when one of the cylinder covers was smashed he had one made of wood.

George Grenfell was born at Ennis Cottage, Sancreed, near Penzance on 21st August 1849, son of George Grenfell of Trannack Mill and his wife Joanna, daughter of Michael and Catherine Rowe of Botrea, Sancreed. In 1852/3 George, brother John and sister Mary were taken by their parents to live in Birmingham.

As he grew up, young George became attached to the Heneage Street Baptist chapel in Birmingham and felt the call to become Missionary. The loss of an eye in early life in no way impaired his energy. In September 1873, influenced by the life of David Livingstone, Grenfell entered the Baptist College in Bristol and on 10th November 1874 the Baptist Missionary Society accepted him. He spent thirty-two years in Africa; the first three years in the Cameroons and the remaining years in the Congo.

George Grenfell married Mary Hawkes in Birmingham in 1876. Within 12 months she had died in the Cameroons.

In 1878 he married Rose Patience Edgerley, an African bride who accompanied him in many of his adventurous journeys. The Royal Geographical Society published his chart of the Congo basin and awarded him its Founder's Medal in 1887. In 1891 the King of the Belgians and Sovereign of the Congo State presented him with the insignia of Chevalier of the Order of Leopold. In 1906 he died in the country which he had done much to civilise.

Mary Grenfell

Mary Marks (nee Grenfell), George Grenfell's sister was a widow when she married Hannibal Rowe of Trevean after his first wife, Margaret Jane nee Pengelly, died in 1905. Hannibal and Mary retired to Trannack Mill.

John Grenfell

John, George's brother, became a watchmaker and jeweller. On retirement he came back to Ennis with his wife Emma.

Ennis and Trannack Mill belonged to him, also some cottages in Chapel Place. He turned one of those cottages into a READING ROOM and people would go there to read the 'Dailies'. He sold Ennis in 1927/8. He is buried in Sancreed Churchyard – (up the steps and under the yew tree to the right of the path). His niece, Carrie Grenfell is buried in the same grave, although there is no tombstone.

TRANNACK MILL

Hugh Rowe: "From my boyhood days, I was fascinated by the sight and sound of a traction engine, and fate seemed more than kind to me when I started work in 1926 for the Hosking family at St Buryan, who were among the pioneers of steam threshing contractors in this district."

As a farm worker Hugh Rowe did all the usual farm work, ploughing, cultivating and harvesting with horses. Also hedging and milking at Boskennal, but when autumn came

St Buryan Male Voice Choir.
Back Row from left: John Hutchings, John Jackson, George Ellis, Herbert Hutchings, Ben Hocking.
Middle Row: John Williams, Leslie Cargeeg, Geoffrey Semmens, Frank Hall, Ken Hall, Donald Bolitho, John Jackson, Leonard White, John Williams, Bill Ellis.
Front Row: John Evans, Clarence Evans, Willie Lugg, Hugh Rowe (conductor), Ernie Hall (president), Mildred Angwin (accompanist), Bill Nicholls, Gerald Male, William Jackson.

he was out with the traction engine, which he drove for Warwick Hosking, taking the threshing machine and trusser from farm to farm to thresh the corn and tie the straw in bundles. Later he drove for Lewis Hosking.

He married Miriam in June 1939. At Christmas 1940 with a group of men he went out singing carols for the Red Cross. So began the St Buryan Male Voice Choir, which has continued for 67 years with Hugh Rowe as the first conductor. The choir has had a whole lifetime of giving pleasure and raising money for a great many good causes along the way by singing in churches and chapels, (including it seems, Drift, Newbridge, Sancreed, Brane, Trevarthen and Tregerrest chapels as well as Sancreed Church), village halls and some very illustrious venues, including the Tower of London.

Hugh was threshing at Mr Harry Trewern's farm at Trewey, St Levan on 20th October 1942 and his wife Miriam was expecting their first child. At midday he had a telephone message reporting the birth of Melville.

The news quickly spread and later after being away for a while he returned to find the engine canopy decorated from stem to stern with hydrangeas and other flowers.

At Trannack Mill
Leslie Oats asked Hugh Rowe to manage Trannack Mill Farm, and Hugh, Miriam, and their four young boys went there in 1955 until 1970.

On Sunday mornings, when they went to chapel, those boys, Melville, Donald, Leslie and Geoffrey (Jethro) were turned out to perfection, a credit to their mother. They used to go to chapel in the morning, Sunday school in the afternoon and chapel in the evening. On an occasion, those two young boys Leslie and Jethro had white mice in their pockets when they went to chapel. In the middle of the sermon they let those mice go! Those two boys were always in trouble.

Leslie, Melville and Donald Rowe.

Memories of my father "Hugh Rowe"

Melville Rowe: "My father was a kind man who never judged people and was always caring towards them. He was a true "Christian" for 7 days a week. He was a very talented man and as young children he made all our Christmas presents. Also models of steam engines, which were indeed exciting for us all.

He also possessed a steam engine (model), which he found and restored. He would use it to power the many examples of fairground rides we constructed from our Meccano Sets. I recall when we lived at Penzance Road, St Buryan that our back garden was full of swings, roundabouts and seesaws mainly constructed from the crossmembers of telegraph poles.

He kept goldfish in the back kitchen window and changed the water once a week. On one occasion he slipped and smashed the glass receptacle and all the fish were sliding around the floor. I think most were saved in the washing up bowl!

Dad enjoyed life to the full - his family, his many friends, his church and his choir. I was extremely proud of him."

Four sons

His four sons are well known in different ways. Melville, like his father, became the conductor of a male voice choir – Tintagel. Donald has a chimney sweep business, Leslie is the landlord of two pubs, The Peruvian and The Dock Inn in Penzance and Geoffery (Jethro) is a famous Cornish comedian.

Jethro has a haircut

Leslie Rowe: "Geoff (Jethro) was supposed to have his haircut. He was seventeen and driving by this time.

Dad said, "If you don't have your haircut on Saturday you are not going out". He came back. He hadn't had it cut. He said, "I am having it cut on the way over to see my girlfriend. It will be cut". I went out to help dad with the milking on Sunday morning. I looked at Geoff in the bed. He had not had his haircut. I said, "You're going to be in trouble mate". He said, "I know".

Dad went to chapel that morning. "You're going to have to cut my hair for me. Father is going to kill me if I don't have my hair cut". I tried to cut his hair, made a huge mess of it. We were in real trouble now. We didn't want Mum to see it so we got Geoff out of the bedroom window and took him up to the old factory, to Mrs. Boase who was a hairdresser. "Can you do anything with that Mrs. Boase? She said, "Not very much. You've made a real mess of his hair". She had to cut it really short to cover the marks I had made with the scissors.

Father came back from chapel. We all sat down for dinner. He looked over his glasses, **"I don't know who cut your hair boy. I wouldn't go there any more!"**

Vanished

Melville Rowe: "We used to go to Sancreed chapel and the pews were elevated from the front to the back. The back row of pews had a door in from the steps. One evening service I was late and father and mother were already sitting in the pew in the front of the back row by the stairs. During the week the caretaker had lifted the manhole, which was directly inside the door from the top of the steps. This was done to air under the elevated seats. I walked smartly up the stairs opened the door and fell down through the manhole to a depth of some five feet. Father heard the bump and turned around to find me "gone" I was able to climb out and get singing the second verse!"

Hugh Rowe, a man of many accomplishments, passed away in 1992

In boyhood days when doing fractions
He dreamed in school of driving tractions
And soon the dream was put in action
Proud driver of the 'Taskers' traction.

Another dream, a challenge there,
With stone the boundary hedge repair
In hedging contest left his stamp
And he became a Cornish champ.

Another dream he did aspire
Formation of our Male Voice Choir
So talented, so kindly too
There'll never be another HUGH

BOLEPPA - Sarah Carter & Robin Meneer

Boleppa was probably never a farm. Long ago when this valley was being streamed this must have been the only fording place. Now the stream goes under the road. We have found Bronze Age floors underneath here; also we have found a lot of flints (one flint is amazing, shaped like a knife). For a long time there would have been an old track way and crossroads here; with a well in the garden it could also have been a watering place.

CHAPTER 6

BOTREA AREA - pronounced Botray

It has been written, "Botrea, a farm of about 500 acres, was converted by Col. Scobell of Nancealverne from a howling wilderness into smiling pastures". Celtic author, William Botterell, suggests Botrea means 'the home house or ancestral place'. Also nearby is the deserted Balleswidden Mine, once one of the largest tin mines in Cornwall.

Usticke, Scobell and Armstrong

The reader may like to know a little of the background of the family who had owned so much of Sancreed and had a strong connection with Botrea.

Charles Usticke bought Leah, St Buryan from Major Thomas Grosse who had led a Royalist army against Cromwell's men in the Civil War. Charles' son Oliver married Julian Roscrow an heiress and inherited property in St Just, Mabe, Gluvias, St.Agnes, Redruth, Gwennap and Wendron, which was left to their son William, born at Leah.

He was later known as William Usticke of Holborn and Nancealverne. His daughter Susanna inherited his estate. She married Colonel Scobell and had three children: John Usticke born 1804, (he was farming Cardinney in 1838), George Scobell 1806, and Susanna Scobell 1807. All were baptised at Madron. Judge Scobell Armstrong was a descendent and took charge of the Scobell Armstrong estate in the early 1900s.

Botrea New House, built around the old one while John White and family lived there.

Boyhood days
from 'Yesterday' by His Honor Judge Scobell-Armstrong CBE

"From the time when my grandmother inherited Nancealverne in 1890, it became our holiday home whether we were living on the Continent or in England. In the course of our frequent and prolonged visits to her I acquired an intimacy with farm life in Cornwall which has furnished me with many cherished and indelible memories. As often as I could I cycled out to one or other of the farms belonging to my family, carrying, when I grew older, a gun strapped to my shoulders.

Troublesome though I no doubt often was to the busy occupant I was always sure of a warm welcome, and wandered for hours among the animals and the crops, proud at times to be entrusted with a bit of work, which I probably did badly but with much enthusiasm. Such efforts on my part were interspersed with permitted raids upon the Cornish 'twists' and the cream pan. People who talk about Cornish cream today have little idea of what Cornish cream once was and ought still to be. It was made on a furze fire, which gave it a delicious slightly smoky flavour. It was never violated by a separator and when sufficiently scalded, was transferred in large thick slabs to the cream bowl. Part of it was made into butter which tasted almost the same as the cream itself.

How often in the evening, when the day's work and play were over, I trudged, tired out, up the lane to Botrea, a farm high on a hillside dominating one of the loveliest of Cornish valleys, to be welcomed by the oil-lamp in the window, just lighted and shining as steadfastly as the evening star. What a happy little gathering and what a spread on the kitchen table I found there! The farmhouse evening in those times was a scene that no one with any degree of artistic perception could ever forget-the farmer with his beaming face just in from milking, the housewife bustling to and from the larder in search of fresh provender, the children gloating over their jam and cream, and the dear old Cornish range called the' slab', with its polished brasses, a triumph of strenuous arm work. The conversation was merry and light, but by no means uninstructive, for farmers and their wives, though not indulging in learned words, are capable of embodying a good deal of shrewd practical philosophy in a single sentence."

Henry Thomas Bearded Sage and Estate Agent

"I spent quite a lot of time as I grew older in the company of Henry Thomas. He was the bearded patriarch and sage of St Just, whose mind was a well of knowledge and a treasury of common sense. He had become the agent for Nancealverne Estate in succession to his father, and was reputed to be the greatest living authority on the vocabulary and structure of the ancient Cornish language. No doubt he acquired much of his knowledge of it from his intelligent father. At the time when we celebrated his sixtieth anniversary as our agent a long account of him appeared in the '*Cornishman*', the following passage from which shows the veneration in which he was held in the district"

'Scholars of distinction, not only from this country, but from abroad, have found delight in an afternoon or evening spent with Mr. Thomas at Carvorrow. Among those who frequently consulted him concerning the famous stone circles and other ancient monuments of Cornwall, was the late Sir Norman Lockyer, the eminent scientist, at one time Director of the Solar Physics Observatory, South Kensington. The latter made a point of seeking out and consulting Mr. Thomas when he visited Cornwall.'

"My first drive in a motor-car was along the road by the sea between Penzance and Marazion. The car was a Serpolet, an open contraption with seats on the top of a receptacle that seemingly contained a quantity of powerful machinery. It actually reached, between Penzance and Long Rock, the appalling speed of thirty miles an hour. I clung to my seat expecting every moment to be my last". The car was probably Colonel Paynter's.

Henry Thomas farmer, Land Agent.

Henry Thomas was born at Jericho in 1854 the youngest of seven children. In the latter part of the 1800s, he followed his father as tenant of Botrea Farm. He was as well, for many years, the land agent for the Scobell-Armstrong estate. A self-taught man who went on to become an historian - well versed in the Cornish language.

Henry was the manager of Sancreed Dairy, a Methodist local preacher, involved in planning and building Escalls Chapel (1900), and of Trewellard Sunday School. He was a clerk of the works for St Just Wireless Station etc and for St Just Urban District Council water reservoir. Henry had a seed and fertilizer business in St.Just, became a member of Cornwall County Council from 1898 to 1902 and he was created a Cornish Bard in 1932.

THE HATTAMS OF BOTREA

Henry Hattam (of Boscregan, then Bosavern, St Just)

+

Mary Jane Roberts (of St Just)

Their children:
1. **Everett** b 1888 + May Chirgwin, (children Gwennie and Ernie),
   farmed Lower Botrea
2. **Edith** b 1890 + Richard (Dick) Nicholls, (children Olive, May, Kathleen,
   Harry, Mary), farmed Boslow
3. **May** b 1891 + Edward Thomas White, (one child Ivy),
   farmed at Brane then at Hendra, Cot Valley
4. **Harry** b 1892 + Katie Bottrell, no offspring,
   farmed at Bodinner Vean then Nanquithno, Sancreed
5. **Olive** b and d 1894
6. **Frances** b 1895 + John Oats Lawry (one child Mary d young)
   farmed Nanquithno, Sancreed then Trannack Mill 1920, Sancreed
7. **Belinda** b 1897 + Alfred Lawry (one child, Leonard, d young)
   farmed Myrtle Grove
8. **Gertrude** b 1898 + John Eva White (children, Doris, Clarice and Jack),
   farmed at Brane and.then at Botrea
9. **Mary** b 1902 – did not marry (looked after parents)
10. **Will** b 1903 + Bessie Angwin (children Justus and Grace) own lorry/ milk round.

Life at Botrea- tales told by my father.

Justus Hattam: "My father, William Charles Hattam (1903-1986) was the youngest child of Henry and Mary Jane Hattam. The landlords, the Scobell-Armstrongs, used to give the children gifts at Christmas and I still have a book inscribed and given to Dad by them.

My father told many stories about Botrea. One I remember was about a wagonload of quicklime, hauled by a traction engine and delivered via the Grumbla entrance to Botrea. In crossing the wooden bridge over the river the weight of the traction engine and its load caused the bridge to collapse, sending some of the quicklime into the water. Father remembered the water bubbling and boiling as the quicklime was quenched!

Hunting was productive as a source of food. Young rabbits, called 'grazers', were shot and trapped. These were then skinned, fried with onions and served with thin cream for breakfast, always after milking.

Each farm would help the other at harvest time and workers would come to Botrea from Grumbla, Higher Botrea, Bosence, Leswidden and Jericho. The farm feast or 'Guldise' celebration at the end of harvesting would see the long table in the kitchen laden from end to end with all sorts of food prepared for the harvest workers, pride of place taken by a large piece of roast beef.

'Crowst' for the workers, saffron cake, home made buns and heavy cake washed down by plenty of tea, was carried out to the fields by the girls in large baskets covered in linen cloths.

Remote farms of the area had visiting pedlars who would carry boxes of goods for sale such as matches, candles, shoe-laces, pins, needles, cotton, small utensils and so on. The usual pedlar who came to Botrea was affectionately called 'Granfer Dunn' and Grandmother would always buy something to keep her stocks up. As sweets were not easily come by Dad would make his own brittle toffee by heating butter, sugar and treacle in an empty treacle tin over a candle!

Local events such as feast days, carnivals and village sports were attended with great enthusiasm. Dad was a keen competition cyclist and raced at as many local sports venues as possible. He gained the silver medal in the AAA Five Mile Championship of Devon and Cornwall held in Penzance one year.

Sunday as a day of rest was strictly observed with attendance at Chapel, usually Trevarthen or sometimes Tregerest. Most of the family met their future husbands/wives at chapel, a sign of the importance of religious involvement in their social activities. Only essential jobs such as milking or feeding the livestock were carried out on Sundays.

The corn that was grown for animal feed was a mixture of Cornish Black oats and barley. Corn was sown broadcast by hand in the early years but later on a 'fiddle' was used.

Looking after farm stock and implements was essential and repair was very much the order of the day. Implements were taken to Reynolds, the blacksmith at Newbridge, for repair. A big tub of grease and oil was kept in the barn for protecting tools and implements after use, applied with an old paintbrush.

Dad had to leave school at Sancreed early to work on the farm because his brothers,

Everett and Harry were called up during World War One. As a result of him being so young, when doing harvest work on the farm he would be tied into the seats of the reaper and binder because his legs were too short for his feet to reach the stays!

Hospital visit

On one occasion Dad was told to walk two heifers to Penzance market. On the way past Penzance Hospital they decided to turn right and walk up the hospital steps! No sooner had they been driven out onto the road again than they headed into a private passage way. Dad said he could hear the lady in the house screeching! Grandfather would go to Penzance market on horseback most weeks, travelling via Higher Botrea and the white gate out onto the St Just road by Jericho Farm."

Jean White: "My great grandparents, Henry and Mary Jane Hattam, farmed Botrea from 1907 until 1930 when they retired. Each of their nine surviving children had their own jobs around the farm. My grandmother, May White nee Hattam, worked in the dairy making butter and cream.

My mother told me that Mrs Scobell-Armstrong used to praise great grandmother for her bacon and said it was the best she had ever tasted. Great granny used to say, "Little does she know, I always keep the best for us!"

My grandmother lived at the cottage at Botrea when I was very little and I remember she had a well just outside the front door, covered with a slate, from which she drew all her water. In the drought of the 1970s, when there was talk of pumping water from the clay works, just beyond Botrea land, to boost mains supplies, granny was beside herself as she reckoned we'd all be poisoned from the arsenic in the pits there!"

Doris, Jack and Clarice White.

John White and his Family

In 1930 John and Gertie White with their children Doris, Clarice and Jack moved from a farm at Brane to Botrea to take over when Gertie's parents retired. (Gertie was a daughter to Henry and Mary Jane Hattam)

Norah Pearce: "For 2 years they lived as best they could whilst the 'new' house was built around the 'old' house. Ultimately a fine house resulted which had an Aga cooker and a big boiler alongside in the kitchen, which also had a long table that could seat about twenty people. Uncle Jack had been poorly for quite a while and when the doctor came to see him, gran (Gertie White) died suddenly by his bedside. Grandpa (John White) had a stroke after gran died and Jack carried on with the farm until he retired in about 1966.

He went on a cruise and met his wife Eva, a New Zealand lady, and they had a daughter, Judith, when he was 50."

Everett, May, Gwennie & Ernie Hattam

LOWER BOTREA

Everett and May Hattam (nee Chirgwin) farmed at Lower Botrea from about 1928. They had two children, a daughter Gwennie, who married Willie Grose and farmed at Bosvargus, St Just and a son, Ernie, who carried on the farm after his parents' death until he himself died in 1986 aged 60. He was a very keen cricketer, organized euchre and whist drives and with the help of his mother organised the dances at Sancreed Institute. When the riding school started Ernie's mother was worried that these very attractive girls were going to get hold of Ernie. He never married!

HIGHER BOTREA

Ron Prowse: "Just before I was 9 we moved to the larger smallholding of Higher Botrea rented from Judge Scobell Armstrong. This consisted of 25 acres, plus the 80 acres of Botrea Hill we used for rough grazing. It was part of the larger Botrea Farm and sublet to us by farmer John White. Money was needed to build up the farm's live and dead stock so my father continued working at Newlyn Quarry where he had become employed when the clay works started closing in 1935. He worked there until a road accident in 1939 put paid to his travelling.

It took several years to improve the fields which had been neglected due to the ill-health of elderly Mr Lawry and we all had to help out to bring some of the fields back into cultivation. It meant working-out a large amount of stroil (couch grass root) and burning it in scores of small heaps scattered all over the fields. Financially times were hard and there was considerable doubt over whether I could attend the County School in Penzance after passing the scholarship in 1938. As it was when the opportunity arose to go on an excursion to Windsor in 1939 costing 10s (50p) I had to choose between it and a new satchel. I chose the latter!

Botrea Mine.

Trials and Tribulations

Botrea Stairs factory at Higher Botrea.

Times were hard for most people but we were mostly in the same boat and the phrase "keeping up with the Jones's" was unknown to us; it was more a case of keeping one's head above water.

My parents had a particularly difficult time because of problems with the cattle due to contagious abortion, mastitis and several cases of wooden tongue in which the cows had difficulty feeding and their milk yields fell off seriously. In a few short weeks we also lost 100 laying hens, half of our flock, to daytime raids by foxes.

Over the years a rumpus at night meant that a fox had got into a hen house through a pophole left open or, on occasion, a badger that had broken in by ripping off boarding to gain entry which foxes did not do. Foxes would have a killing spree but badgers tended to make off with two or three to feed their young. In either case the noise resulted in a dash downstairs, a quick grab of the 12 bore and out to the hen house in the hope of catching the intruder inside. It was a case of their survival or ours! Fortunately for us, in about 1933 the Milk Marketing Board had been set up giving a guaranteed price for milk and the monthly milk cheque was a lifeline.

The situation in those days meant that everyone on farms had to work from the age of 10 or so and Saturdays and holidays saw me and other farmer's sons doing various jobs around the farm including working the horses in the fields, feeding calves, putting food in the cribs, chopping Swedes etc, planting potatoes and cabbages and hoeing.

There was always a job which needed doing. Everyone learned to hand milk the cows but I was never called on to do this in the morning though I knew of many at school and my cousins who were. By the age of 12 or so we were capable of harnessing the horses and using them to prepare the ploughed fields for seed sowing and I remember on a cold, dry, windy morning in March or April how grateful I was to get a flask of hot cocoa brought out to the field where I was working. Even more welcome than the NAAFI van later on when in the Army!

Watching the Blacksmith at work

At one time I was lucky to be able to see the construction of our new cob cart by Tommy Grenfell with ironwork made by Willy Reynolds (and sons). The cart was made completely from bare timber, selected as was required, particularly for the specialist parts such as the shafts and wheels.

I was told that if I came down from school on a specific day I could watch the iron 'bind' or 'tyre' being shrunk on to the wooden wheel. This was a job for all three of the blacksmiths to position the 5 ft diameter hoop, (that had been heated to a full red heat), accurately and in unison to drop it in place and then very quickly to quench it before the wooden rim became too scorched.

As the seasons came round so too did the jobs. After field preparation, crops were sown or planted, potato planting being the least loved, and their subsequent lifting was no less back breaking. In wet seasons both jobs were mucky but on average the weather in spring and again in early summer was not too unkind. Not so the growing period when the frosts often damaged the tender leaves and late spring gales could strip the developed leaves severely and destroy the crop.

During the war we were required to grow certain acreage. This was a lucrative cash crop and was an important part of our income and also of pocket money for those of my school friends I could persuade to join in the work.

Graf Zeppelins

In the early 1930s, somewhat out of the usual were the sightings of the huge German airships flying over West Penwith. We were lucky to see these twice in about 1933. I well remember one of these giant airships proceeding majestically overhead in the early evening travelling slowly from the south-west to the north-east at what must have been about 1000 feet returning from the USA to Germany. I think that it was the Graf Zeppelin but it may have been the ill-fated Hindenberg

With the magic of the circus, the fairground with its huge gleaming traction engines and enormously extravagant rides crammed into a small area filled with people and the occasional momentous occasion together with an exciting working environment I am grateful to have been born in the first quarter of the 20th century.

Handling accounts

At home and at school it is worth noting the trust placed in many of us from a young age and our freedom from fear of such things as being mugged or otherwise interfered with though this is not to say that we never got into fights or that we never misbehaved. However from the age of six I was sent on my bike with the appropriate money from Boslow down to Bennetts shop at Trewellard to pay the bills for animal and poultry feed.

At school our teacher's monthly salary was paid into their account at Barclays Bank in St Just and, presumably with prior agreement, one of us pupils would be sent to withdraw some cash. Most transactions in those days were with cash or by cheque. At the age of 10 or so we would be put on the bus outside school and at St Just would go to the bank, do the business, put the cash envelope in our pocket and catch the same bus back to school. As the bus normally had a 5 minute stop at St Just this always worked out. Doubtless, unknown to us, the conductor, all of whom were well known to us, had been apprised of our mission and we were never stranded!

Good neighbours

One lovely Sunday morning in the late 30s or early 40s I was helping my father in the hayfield when John White and his wife passed down the lane going home from morning service. He stopped the car and coming towards us said, "Do you know what day this is Harry?". "Yes," my father replied, "It's a lovely Sunday; I suppose you've been to chapel?" "We have," said John, "it's the Lord's Day and we have been giving praise." "Yes," my father responded, "I've been giving praise as well out here in the field to have been given such a lovely day to help me save my hay."

"I'm sure we must all give thanks for what the good Lord has given us," said John and went on his way. There was no animosity on either side and very shortly after, my father gave a hand at Lower Botrea with the corn harvest.

Good deeds

More tellingly, a few years later when I was in the Army, my father took a tumble from his horse immediately before the critical potato lifting time. On Whit Monday morning at 8am John White, his son Jack, their workman, Reggie Rowe and his workman, and Charlie Oats all turned up at our farm. Together they lifted father's entire crop of potatoes. They were bagged and put by the roadside ready for collection next day.

This was an act of neighbourliness which neither my parents nor I ever forgot. It was the day of the Victory celebration parade through London. Nowadays we would all be watching it on TV. This act meant more to us than the parade in London."

Trinity Rocket Store

Ken Wood (ex-Policeman): "My security visits to explosives stores included the old Trinity House rocket store which was in a remote position at Botrea, adjacent to the rough lane from Jericho Farm to Grumbla (O.S.Grid ref. 401308), Sancreed.

The purpose of Trinity House storing rockets and other pyrotecnics was for warning devices (flares) and lifeline rocket equipment (breeches buoy). This unlit little store was more often than not only guarded by rabbits, but was still listed as a vulnerable premise and required my attention. Local farmers would stand in wonder at my occasional wandering up the hill."

Trinity rocket store.

Sancreed Sailors

Ron Prowse: "With some beaches reopened and Mount's Bay once more open for small boats up to 5 of us would join schoolmate Bill Turner in his 15ft drop keel sailing dinghy to sail and fish there.

In 1944, Bill was going away for the Whitsun holiday and offered me the use of his boat and this time the risk was all mine with no one else to blame. I enlisted cousin Donald Liddicoat as crew and he brought along friend Clifford Pollard (son of Joe Pollard, the postman). As Sea Cadets I considered them experienced sailors. We were out of Penzance harbour not long after one o'clock, set sail and dropped the keel and with a nice westerly breeze in no time we were well to the south of the Mount and then past Perranuthnoe and on to Cudden Point.

By this time a breeze started to freshen and the sea was looking pretty vast. By mutual consent we decided that it was time to go about and start tacking for home. After three attempts and three near capsizes I realised that my crew were no more skilled than I, so we very quickly dropped the sail, lifted the keel and started rowing with two at the oars and one resting.

If we stopped rowing for an instant it was obvious that we were going out to sea; the freshening offshore wind and the ebbing tide were both against us and rain was not far off! We kept hard at it and eventually well over 3 hours later to our great relief we made it to the lee of Penzance harbour aching and sore everywhere especially on our thighs and rumps and with badly blistered hands. Climbing up the harbour side ladder and cycling home that night were further hard labour and not a fish for tea! To add to my woe, a few days later confessing to Bill he merely said "You idiot, why didn't you put into the Mount? I was unable to swim and I doubt if my crew were very proficient, we had no life jackets, no one knew we were out there Our parents were never told."

At Donald Liddicoat's Golden Wedding Dinner in 2008 Ron was telling Donald's grandson this story when his neighbour piped up "I was there". It was Clifford Pollard who Ron had not met since that time over 60 years ago!

BOSENCE

The Bosence family settled at Sancreed in 1290, and for long centuries its members married almost exclusively into other families long established in West Cornwall. During the 17th and 18th centuries there were fifty-six Bosence weddings in Cornwall, all in West Penwith. More than half of them were at Sancreed.

By 1951 the name of Bosence was reduced to ten persons distributed between Penzance, Sancreed and Camborne.

This was caused partly by emigration. Richard Bosence of Trevorian, migrated to Victoria with his wife soon after their marriage at Sancreed in 1854. Their ship, the Parsee (1172 tons, Captain E. E. Thomas), left Plymouth on 27th February and arrived in Melbourne on 9th June. The passengers included William Henry Bosence, Thomas James and their respective wives who were the sisters Mary and Matilda, formerly Matthews. Upon arrival William Henry Bosence was given employment at Geelong by a Mr Matthews.

In the 1600s, a great part of Sancreed belonged to the ancient family of Bosence. Around that time there is mention of Uter Bosence (pronounced Ooter) and his son Uter a champion wrestler, and again 200 years later another Uter Bosence a noted hurler.

Lockheed Hudson bomber crashes into Farmhouse
(interview with Claud Bottrell)

Farmer John Hosken and his wife moved into the newer farmhouse at Bosence in 1940. This had been built for Scobell Armstrong in 1936.

A few weeks later on the 7th November at 8.20pm, after hitting the stable, a Lockheed Hudson bomber, crashed at high speed into the old Bosence Farmhouse

Bosence, house destroyed by crashed plane.

which it almost demolished. It turned up side down and an engine careered on past the house down through the field beyond and into a moor below. By this time the Hudson was on fire.

The crew of four had abandoned the plane when they discovered that they were lost and landed by parachute. One had apparently jumped at 90ft, and was lucky to be alive. He got to the farmhouse and was given a cup of tea. He was minus a boot which he had lost on the way down! The entire cordage of the parachute with the World War Two flying boot was found 66 years later, in 2006 when they were ploughed up by the farmer Claud Bottrell's son James. Claud's father, William Bottrell, had been with the Home Guard on the Beacon at the time and they came to check the plane. They had thought a 'Jerry' had landed.

Apparently two bombs had been released from the plane and exploded later, one in the sheepwalk up near the farm boundary, the other in the lane above the farmyard. The story goes that Farmer John Hosken touched it or kicked it and a short time later it exploded.

The Hudson was used for maritime recognizance and was a part of a Canadian flight of three Hudson Medium bombers, probably returning from a sortie and seemingly were unsure of their position and could not get permission to land at either Portreath or Predannack due to enemy activity.

Nothing remains of the old farmhouse or the plane. A new house is being built on the site. When digging the foundations long belts of 303 pellets were discovered.

Claud Bottrell with cordage of parachute, ploughed up after 67 years.

Norah (daughter of Reggie Rowe and Doris nee White, formally of Botrea) and Roger Pearce's wedding.

Bombs again

Just over two years later on 16th Feb1943 four high explosive bombs dropped on grassland at Bosence Farm Sancreed. Two exploded and two did not. Two incendiary bombs dropped at the same time.

After the War John Hosken retired to Feock and William Bottrell (Claud's father) rented Bosence Farm.

In the garden of the present farmhouse there is a millstone cut for a bone mill but unused. A mill nearby was used to grind up bones for fertilizers.

Grandfather Richard Bottrell served his time at the blacksmiths shop at Buryas Bridge. He shod all the ponies at Geevor Mine for some time. He walked there and rode the skip down the mine, then walked back home again in the evening. When he married he farmed at Tresvennack, Paul and came to farm Lower Bodinnar in1919.

From wartime Police Notes.

In August 1941 a British Hurricane fighter crashed at Watering Place Sancreed. The machine was completely wrecked but not burnt and the occupant died as a result of the crash.

Bombs at Bosvenning and Roskennels Farm, Newbridge. Three exploded one unexploded.

On 6th Sept 1941 two para mines dropped and exploded in grass fields at Tregonebris, Considerable damage to farm house and buildings.

At the end of January 1942 a light balloon was found in a field at Botrea.

Balleswidden Mine
Earthquakes and Explosion

Cornish Telegraph 21st November 1842

"A fatal accident occurred at this mine [Balleswidden] yesterday week; G Gilbert, of Sancreed, when about to enter the ladders, was struck on the head by a large stone, which fell from a chasm of some considerable height. The unfortunate man died on the following morning, having lingered until that time quite insensible."

Balleswidden Mine was established on soft ground, the bedrock granite being extensively kaolinised. This led to there being many collapses and falls of rock, the biggest recorded in 1845 caused a depression of about 270 feet long, over 42 feet wide and over 12 feet deep which could be seen at the surface. It has also been recorded that during its history, the mine suffered a series of **minor earthquakes**!

This mine on the St Just Road right on the boarder of Sancreed and St Just parishes, employed many Sancreed men and boys. Between 1831 and 1914 there were at least 42 recorded deaths as a result of collapses and rock falls, although not all deaths by these causes were recorded.

Cornish Telegraph 21st November 1866

"SAD ACCIDENT – An accident, which ended fatally to a lad named Benjamin Thomas, about 12 years of age, happened on Monday at Balleswidden Mine. The poor fellow was underground and fetching some water in a box, when a piece of ground gave way, and so crushed his head and chest that he died from the effects of the injuries the following night."

It was reported in the *Mining Journal* on 2nd January 1841 that as several men were in the boiler house of Balleswidden Mine changing their clothes, a container of **gunpowder exploded**, badly scalding seven miners and badly damaging the roof.

Between 1856 and 1857 Balleswidden used an experimental and revolutionary system of gas, instead of candles, to illuminate various sections of the mine but this was not extended to other mines nor continued at Balleswidden.

JERICHO

Norah Pearce: "Around 1928 Reggie Rowe came to Jericho with his parents from Relubbus. He married Doris White from Botrea and I was their only child.

At the end of the war tractors were very scarce and names were put into a hat. Father was lucky. He was able to buy that Fordson tractor on spade lugs. No tyres then!

On our last threshing day we were 40 people who sat down to dinner. It was a social occasion. We had a great Tag of beef and apple tart. We also took crowst out to the men both mid morning and late afternoon. A kettle of tea, a kettle of camp coffee and heavy cake etc.

I drove the Ferguson tractor to cut corn with the binder when I was seven. We used to stand the sheaves up, 8 sheaves to a shock and then build them into mows each of 8 shocks. Later we would often buckrake them to the threshing machine.

The men used to build the straw bundles into ricks which were then thatched. My job was to take the rope of coir yarn on a long pole to the men at each end tying the thatch down. Later father had his own combine harvester and baler. He was very mechanical and was able to do his own repairs having his own workshop. I cut hay with the tractor and later would sweep it to the rick. The men then forked it into the Lister elevator.

We kept a herd of Guernsey cows. I milked with the milking machine starting at 5.30am and again in the evening.

We had our own water supply pumped up by two rams working night and day requiring no fuel, just a rocking motion of water filling and emptying in the stream. No maintenance. No cost. Occasionally father repaired the rubber flange.

We had no mains electricity but used a lister Startomatic.

We celebrated the Coronation in 1953. I can see it all now the flags, tea and games, and a Coronation mug for every child with a picture of the Queen on it.

I went to Madron Young Farmers Club and took part in the many activities, field days, County Rallies. It was lovely. I met my husband there. Roger was a member of St Hilary YFC."

Bog Inn

In Bostraze Moor, there formerly stood a 'hovel', which went by the name of the 'Bog Inn'. This appears to have been a courtesy title only, since it is doubtful if it had ever received a licence of any sort. Between the years 1850-55 its owner was a man of jovial character who was in the habit of providing sport for the youths of Sancreed and St Just on Sundays by offering prizes for any one who could catch a greased pig, which was let loose amidst the banks and pools of the surrounding tin stream works. This sport created much enjoyment for everyone (except the unfortunate animal). The pig was only caught after a long chase. It also had the effect of creating a unwonted thirst among the ' sportsmen', for whose benefit supplies of porter and smuggled spirit were fetched from the neighbouring town of St Just, and found a ready sale.

Bog Inn.

On the St Just boundary of Jericho Farm, the remains of the Bog Inn, covered in ivy are still visible.

'John Thomas & the ghost', from the Arminion Magazine

"A few days ago I visited John Thomas, of St Just, in Cornwall. He is about sixty-two years of age, and has been a notorious drunkard the greatest part of his life. He told me that on Sunday, 21st December 1783, about 7 o'clock in the evening he left San Crete (now spelt Sancreed) in order to go to St Just. As it was dark he missed his way, and about midnight fell into a pit about five fathoms deep. On his being missing his friends made diligent search for him, but to no purpose. The next Sabbath day, as one of his neighbours was going to seek his sheep; he saw, at some distance, the appearance of a man sitting on the bank which had been thrown up in digging the pit. On drawing near he saw the apparition go round to the other side of the bank. When he came to the place he could see no one; but heard a human voice in the bottom of the pit. Thinking that some smugglers had got down to hide their liquors, he went on; but coming back the same way he again heard the voice. He now listened more attentively, and as he could hear but one voice he concluded it was John Thomas who was missing, and on calling to him he found that he was not mistaken. On this he went and got help, and soon got him out of the pit. But as he had been there near eight days he was very low when he was got out; but is now in a fair way to do well. In the bottom of the pit he found a small current of water; which he drank freely of. This, in all likelihood, was the means of keeping him alive. It is said that several other persons saw the apparition, but took no notice of it."

DERVAL

Clarence Hosken: "We were farming there from 1945 to 1985. Muriel and I were married in 1947 and our daughter Gwendoline was born in 1948. We moved into the house that year. Both house and farm were in a run-down state and people thought we were mad to take it on.

The previous tenant was Willie Jenkin who lived there with his wife, son and two sisters. That family had lived there for very many years and Willie's father before them. They used to draw their water from a well just outside the back door by winding it up with a chain and bucket. We had a hand pump fitted in the back kitchen to pump the water in.

Muriel: "We hadn't been there very long when a Ministry man came round 'I'm an inspector, come to check the water you drink here'. He took a sample and came back a few days later. 'You should'nt be drinking that water, its full of bacteria'. I said, 'The previous tenants were drinking that water for nearly 70 years, and they all lived to an old age'. In dry times we had to get our water from a well down the lane. The cattle drank water from the river."

Clarence: "We were delighted when mains water came along. Leslie Oats, our landlord said, 'You supply the labour, I'll supply the pipes'. Gerald Male, the plumber came along with the mole plough and Hugh Rowe our neighbour helped us. We tore down the hedges for the tractor and mole plough to pass through, and then built them up again. Then we helped Hugh do the same at Trannack Farm."

Muriel: "When I married I brought along 60 pullets. They laid like machines. The land not having had poultry well suited them. I kept ducks, and roosters for the Christmas market, and eventually had also 100 laying hens.

We had started farming with very little money and this successful poultry enterprise helped us to get on our feet. We had had no trouble with foxes up to this time, but one day when I was across the valley sweeping hay in with the tractor. I saw feathers flying, and by the time they finished they had killed the lot, a 100 white pullets. The foxes came back for them from all directions, and kept coming. I shot one of them. We gave up poultry keeping after that.

We grew early potatoes. In the dark evening we would be in the barn with a tilley lamp cutting the early potatoes in two ready to plant next day by hand. 3 months later in early June we would be picking up potatoes again all by hand. This crop would be followed by Marrowstem and Hungry gap kale planted with a hand drill. So much of farming used to be hand work."

Newbridge Cricket Team.
Standing from left: Wilfred Oates, Stephen Berryman, Jimmy Lanyon, John Lawry, Clarence Hosking, ? ?, Ruby Elliott, Phil Pengelly, Francis Lanyon, George Lawry, William John Hosken, Ronnie Oats, Donald Prowse, ? Merrifield.
Middle Row (seated): John Eddy, J. H. Hosking, Leslie Oates, James Stevens, Frank Martin.
Seated on grass: Robert Lanyon, Cecil Merrifield, Bernard James.

Cricket

Clarence: "I played cricket for Sancreed for about 15 years. One day I was talking to Mike Giles, Mr Merrifield, and Leslie Oats. I said "Its time to stop this. I've been going home Saturday nights to milk 20 or 30 cows but now I go home to milk 60 or 70, I'm finishing after this season". The others said, 'If you're finishing so are we" and that ended Sancreed cricket.

When Hugh gave up farming in 1968 we were offered Trannack Farm, then Newham and Grumbla. We had started with 70 acres and when we retired we had been farming 190 acres with 80 to 90 cows."

Viv on Warnigal with the cup for best hunter at Newbridge.

Derval Riding School

Sandra James: "Pamela and Vivian Hawken were trained riding school instructors and took the lease on Derval from Mr Leslie Oats in the late 50s.

They acquired 12-16 horses and ponies; some were on loan from other people such as M L Oats and Duncan Simpson of Simpson Bros Penzance. Greville Howard, MP, also kept his mare Williamena there. As well as horses and ponies there was a goat called Silver, a cat by the name of Pussyn and 3 dogs Sputty, Kylie and Shula. Silver was walked twice a day with great difficulty.

Private individuals came for lessons or just a ride out. Penzance private schools came all Saturdays during term time for lessons and were collected from Tremethick Cross in Pam & Vivs's old van. In 1960 they took on two working pupils, Carolyn Harris from St Ives and Sandra Morley from St Just. Carolyn lodged with them but Sandra rode a bike to and fro St Just every day. Their training took 18 months where they then took their B.H.S instructors exams at Bodmin Stud Farm.

Viv Hawken on Hydroplane.

Viv & Carolyn attending St Just Feast.

114

Sandra then left to work with Melville Lawry's show horses at Varfell, Pam then to get married and have a family, although she did return later for a short time. Carolyn stayed on with Viv to run the stables. When finally Viv married the business was sold to Major Hill who moved everything to Little Receven, Newbridge.

Pam, Viv and the two girls enjoyed the local shows in the summer time and hunting with the Western Hounds in the winter months. During one summer Pam, Viv, Margaret Rose Harvey and Sandra entered some carnivals, St Just being one of them.

Vanessa Oats: Leslie Oats, kindly built them 4 loose boxes but provided no grazing, which always proved difficult. Ponies were sometimes tethered on Bartinney Moors for grazing!

A gang of Saturday children enjoyed wonderful times there taking part in summer camps and gymkhanas and making friendships, which have lasted over the years.

Madness in May

During the winter of 1960 the girls were invited to put on a play for Sancreed feast in the village hall in the May of 1961. Pam & Viv's elder sister Joan, a drama teacher, took charge of rehersals which began at Derval and later at Bosence Farm in a barn where Mrs Botterell kindly kept us going with tea and cake.

The play 'Madness in May' was a story about a nutty Professor and his mad housekeeper. Taking part were Sheila Carne, Elizabeth Williams, Tommy James, Vivien Hawken, Sandra Morley, George Shattock, Pamela Hawken, Margaret Adams, Claud Bottrell and Carolyn Harris.

The play was a great success.

Leslie and Jethro take a dip

At Trannack Mill Sancreed lived Hugh and Miriam Rowe with their 4 sons, Melville, Donald, Leslie and Geoffrey (Jethro). The younger two loved walking up to the stables in order to tease the girls and tell their latest jokes.

One day the boys wanted a ride on Sandra's new Raleigh Rudge bike. After much to do it was finally agreed they could ride as far as Mrs Oats's top stables; in other words down the hill and back. Well it didn't happen like that; gathering speed down Trannack Mill lane and unknown to them their father had closed the gate and the two boys ended up in the river. Eventually Hugh arrived at the riding school with the boys in his car and an apology was made. It was decided to buy a new bicycle exactly the same. In theory same bike same colour (white) but it was never the same as the old one somehow."

WHEAL BULLER

Wheal Buller used to be a mine, in earlier days called West Wheal Buller. It was possibly named after General Rt Hon Sir Redvers Buller VC who was credited with having saved Natal from the Boers. The mine operated as Wheal Buller from 1861 until 1873.

Of later years William Richard Williams, Joyce Cargeeg's grandfather farmed the property. By the mid 1960s it was a private house.

CHAPTER 7

TREGEREST AREA

BOSLOW

Ronald Prowse: " I was born in 1926 at the family farm Higher Bostrase in St Just parish. On my father's side the Prowses can directly be traced back to one Robert Prowse born St Buryan in 1715. Early in the 19th C our branch 'emigrated' from St Buryan to the Paul area and split between stone/monumental masons and farmers. By the mid-19thC the stonemasons owned two fine-grain granite quarries on Kerris moor (one painted by Lamorna Birch c. 1910) Before my 6th birthday we moved to Boslow across the moor on the Pendeen road and in Sancreed parish. We rented a cottage with 7 or 8 meadows and a few acres of moorland from the Tregothnan Estate (Lord Falmouth). Here we kept 2 or 3 cows, a few sheep, some pigs and 60 or so hens and ducks. One day my mother witnessed a stampede of our sheep when a circus elephant passed along to Pendeen walked by the circus from Penzance. She last saw them disappearing at speed over the top of the Dry Carn and father had later to go on horseback to round them up.

The holding was better known by its roadside cottage, now our cowshed, from its name, known by all including bus conductors as "Five Old Hats". It was the accepted name of the adjacent bus stop and arose from the old lady who was its last resident having the practice of replacing broken panes of glass in her windows with her discarded old hats! Just by the cottage and built into the hillside is a (pigs') "crow". This was the name given to any such rough animal shelter.

From Boslow I attended Newbridge School two miles away as did the Nicholls family, one boy and four girls, all older than me, some by several years. I went by bus but they usually walked as we all did on Sunday to Tregerest Chapel, a mile away.

With my school friends some distance away, as an only child I spent a lot of time on my own with the two dogs, the aptly named Rover, a collie, and Spot, our hunting terrier. If let off his chain the former could disappear for days in amorous pursuits and return home worn out and sheepishly bearing the scars of battle with other male "rovers". He continued doing this into old age after we moved to Botrea and had been sighted many miles away from home!

Almost a mile up from the village of Newbridge beside the road to the south stands Tregerest Chapel which had the honour of having the village's only burial ground still in use today. 100 yds beyond the chapel the first of two forks led to the North-west and Pendeen. This first fork was a road of considerable antiquity and is far superior to what was necessary to serve Higher Tregerest farm some 200 yds on. It is a very wide, well~laid stone roadway leading over the Dry Carn and so avoiding the marshy area to the south. Though Dry Carn may be derived from Tri Cairn no trace of these remain, whereas Botrea Hill (pronounced Botray and known locally as Barrow Downs), and Derval Downs to the south, there were several barrows and the four on Botrea are quite large and are quite visible today. Another ancient site dating from the Bronze Age on this southern high moorland block lies on the south slope of Trannack Hill. It is variously described as a settlement or as a castle and was first recorded in modern times by W Borlase in 1740 but was even then a ruin. It is named Chirgwidden (Vean) and is believed to date from the Bronze Age.

A mile beyond Tregerest is the parish boundary with Madron on Woon Gumpas (The Gump) and a little further to the west is the Morvah boundary. On the left hand road again a little over a mile from Tregerest is the parish boundary with St Just where the road rises up to another moor by the clay works which is shown on old maps and was known by us in the 30s as The Gooney, also Cornish for moorland."

In the early 1800s Billy Frost used to go round to the feasts in the neighbouring parishes and be well entertained at the public-houses for the sake of his drolls:

UP BOSLOW

"As I traversed Boslow I saw an old cow, a hog, and a flock of starved sheep;
Besides an old mare, whose bones were so bare as to make its poor master to weep.
A few acres of ground, as bare as a pound, an old house ready to fall;
Therein was no meat for the people to eat and that was the worst of the all.

No crock, pan, or kittle; no goods much or little, was there in the old house;
No table or chairs, nor bedding upstairs, not as much as to cover a louse.
No grass for the flocks, but a carn of dry rocks which afforded an horrible sight.
If you pass that way, you must do it by day, for you'd scat your brains in the night!"

That was a long time ago and very sad, but it is very different there now!

BOSWENS - Windy dwelling

How my family came to Boswens.

John Trewern: "In 1911 Grandfather William Henry Trewern snr. born in 1879, sailed to America to see if the prospects were good enough to send home for his family, but

before the end of summer decided he didn't like America and came home. In 1913 he took the tenancy of the most northerly farm in Sancreed parish called Boswens.

Uncle Willie Trewern and Father (Johnny Trewern), when they came to Boswens, had to walk the two miles to Newbridge School.

A new bungalow was built at Boswens for my parents when they married. Mother's family

Boswens.

were farming Nanpean at Cape Cornwall at that time. She always missed the view of the sea.

Father and Uncle Willie farmed the two parts of Boswens separately. When the Milk Marketing Board was set up in 1933 a drawback in Boswens was that the milk had to be taken to a collection point at Bodinnar every day by horse and cart, so they took turns doing alternate days.

I started to walk to school at the age of five.

I now live and farm at Trehyllys, Bosullow but still farm Lower Boswens as an off farm".

Bombs

Incendiary bombs were dropped on Boswens Common on 16th February 1943 and caused gorse fires over 50 acres. On that same night bombs were dropped on Bosence Farm. About the same time many propaganda leaflets, in French, were dropped between Trevedran and Lamorna, St.Buryan

Johnny and Mabel Trewern with son John at Boswens.

Firefly aircraft collide

John Trewern: "On 7th April 1954 My father, Johnnie Trewern, Jimmy Sedgeman and I were digging out a ditch around a field we were about to plant.

Four Firefly aircraft from RNAS Culdrose were in the area practising formation flying as they often did at that time. There was some cloud cover, so from time to time the aircraft disappeared and we took little notice of them. Suddenly there was a rumble from a patch of cloud and we said to each other "What was that? Thunder?" Looking towards the cloud we saw an aircraft diving vertically towards the ground, and when it hit there was a tremendous explosion, with dark red flames and a plume of black smoke.

This was followed by a second aircraft, which had broken up, and appeared to 'flutter' to the ground in at least three pieces, two of which fell on a field of Penhale Farm. We thought there was a small piece of wreckage with a flame streaming behind it. Afterwards we learned it was the pilot of the second aircraft who had either baled out or been thrown.out of his aircraft, the 'flame' being his parachute streaming behind him without opening. Both pilots were killed.

When we first saw the aircraft coming out of the cloud, they appeared to be quite close to us, but in fact hit the ground on Bojuthno and Penhale Farms, a little less than half a mile from where we were working.

Ted Johns the farmer had a narrow escape as he was in the adjoining field driving his Old Standard Fordson Tractor towards the spot where the first aircraft hit the ground.

The wreckage was spread all over that field.

The third aircraft went directly back to Culdrose, whilst the fourth circled the area quite low to direct the rescue services to the crash site. One of the first helicopters I ever saw up close was a Dragonfly, which landed in a field close to the crash site. The road services had the difficult task of coming up the very narrow Bodinnar Lane".

BOJUTHNOE

In the 1950s a young pilot learning to fly flew head on into his instructor's plane. They crashed landed at Bejuthno, and one engine remains 6ft down in that field. See also above

For 30 years after the war Bojuthnoe was farmed by Edward and Grace Johns. Now it is a part of another farm and the farm houses are let.

Dry Carn

What appears to be a very large flying saucer at the top of Dry Carn hill is a communication centre for aircraft coming into this country after crossing the Atlantic. They fix their position from there by radar.

Further down the hill is an aerial providing communication for the coastguard, the police and the mobile phone companies Orange and Vodaphone.

Dry Carn was the old road to Pendeen. The North Road was built between 1840 and 1870.

Where the North Road meets the St Just A3071 was a Toll House. According to the 1881 census the toll collector then was 48-year-old Mary A Bray. Latterly the house has been blown up.

HIGHER TREGEREST

Will Tregear

The Tregears first farmed at Tregerest between 1883 and 1889. John Tregear snr, a miner originally, moved from Bosavern Tenements at St Just to farm at Tregerest with his wife Mary Ann and their children. At some point before 1881, JohnTregear had emigrated to America where two of his children, including the younger John, were born. By 1901, both John Tregear snr and his son, John jnr, were farming at Tregerest.

"The farm at Higher Tregerest has been tested by the existence and endurance of the farmer over 5000 years", states Reg Watkiss, author, who made a

Will Tregear ploughing Higher Tregerest.

cine film of the farming methods of Will Tregear back in the 1960's.

Will Tregear continued farming by 'older' methods, used by both his father and grandfather who worked the hillside previously, more suited to the 19th century than the 20th century. No modern tractor or farming machinery but almost total reliance on a strain of heavy horse bred by his father and grandfather before him. The only concession to 'modern conveniences' was a small generator for pumping.

At the time the film was made, Reg Watkiss commented that the implements on the farm "would enhance a museum" and that the horse-drawn plough was a credit "to good husbandry". When asked how he serviced his farm implements Will Tregear answered, *"I don't do so bad. People I have stuff off are very good to me. Never had no bother"*.

Flat fish across the brambles

The life-style on the farm was also endured by a hard working Mrs Tregear who used to dry her washing like, "flat fish across the brambles" an apt simile used by Reg Watkiss, a custom used over hundreds of years by farmers' wives who believed spreading the washing over the brambles to dry helped kill germs by exposing to the sun the entire item washed. It also had the effect of 'bleaching' the whites.

Locally in the parish there was a saying that you could tell a good ploughman and sower by the measured stride of the farmer. Will Tregear certainly came into this category, working in unison with his horses for ploughing or rolling and his hand sowing rhythmic and steady, his way of life little changed for centuries.

MIDDLE TREGEREST

Leonard & Audrey Harvey nee Giles

About 1830 a family of three brothers Henry, Joseph, and John Giles left a nearby farm at Sancreed and each took a farm in Paul Parish. One of the Giles' family returned to Sancreed 125 years later when John's descendant Audrey Giles married Leonard Harvey in 1952. Of recent years also, two of John Giles' descendants, Audrey's cousins, Mrs Tregear has been farming Higher Tregerest and John Hutchings Lower Tregerest.

Most of the Harveys in West Cornwall appear to descend from a knight Sir Anthony Hervey, whose coat of arms included three harrows. It is said the name derives from harving (harrowing). His son Francis Hervey MA, born 1562 came to Breage in west Cornwall as a priest and, soon after, the family settled at Maen in Sennen. They became very wealthy and owned estates in Sennen, St Buryan and Tolcarne in Newlyn.

Leonard Harvey's family have lived in Sancreed for over 150 years and most of that time at Middle Tregerest.

Two of their sons, Christopher and Michael, between them are farming Higher, Middle, and Lower Tregerest. William is a carpenter.

LOWER TREGEREST

Terry Downes the Champion Boxer

From Joyce Cargeeg: "Terry Downes was aged 4 when he was evacuated to Newbridge with his sister Sylvia aged 7 and cousins Iris and Cissie. They came to stay with the

Williams family at Lower Tregerest. His mother came to see her children but she did not like the countryside and soon went back to her home in London. Iris and Cissie stayed on and went to Newbridge School.

Terry started boxing and soon became a household name. He won the world middleweight title beating Paul Pender.

Terry's sister Sylvia went to America and became a trapeze artist, but unfortunately she lost her arm in a traffic accident. The family went out to support her and while over there Terry joined the U S Marines and became The Golden Gloves Champion. He did not settle there and came back to England. He is still living in London.

He is Britain's oldest living world champion boxer."

Tregerest Chapel

Raymond Tonkin: "A Bible Christian Chapel was built at Newbridge in 1835. This building still stands in the form of the village carpenters shop.

The Wesleyans opened their Newbridge chapel in 1854 and in a short time their following was greater than that of the former. This so disturbed the Bible Christians that they decided to move from Newbridge up the hill and for a time used a 20ft. by 15ft. barn on Middle Tregerest farm in what is now a Cows House as their meeting house. They built a new 'proper' chapel on the main road at Tregerest in 1862. Before then Granny Sampson used to have the class meeting in her sanded kitchen. When she went blind she had it in her bedroom!   The remains of Granny Sampson's little cottage can still be seen in Trannack lane.

In 1892 a 999 year lease was purchased from Cyprian Nicholls of Castallack, Paul, for £5. The Sunday School at the back was built in 1892 and enlarged in 1914.

In 1932 the Bible Christians joined with the Wesleyans and others and from that time were simply known as Methodists.

Granny Anne Boswell, Queen of the Gypsies

Tregerest Chapel has a cemetery and, among others, several gypsies are buried there including Granny Anne Boswell from Helston.

 She was a powerful, feared and mistrusted woman of the Victorian era.   She was married to Ophraim Boswell, King of the Gypsies and they had six children. She hawked her way round West Cornwall, selling potions.

Despite being considered a witch by some people, hundreds attended her funeral in 1909 at Newbridge. The road was lined with gypsy caravans all the way to North Road.

She was buried at the cemetery at Tregerest".

Granny Anne Boswell, Queen of the Gypsies.

Ron Prowse: "In 1896 improvements were made to Tregerest and its graveyard which was the only one in the parish apart from the one at Sancreed Church. In addition to a chapel Tregerest also had a Sunday schoolroom separated by a folding screen so that as well as being used for social functions this room provided extra seating for the special occasions when the congregation would be double that on a normal Sunday or more, totalling as many as two hundred.

At Tregerest the second schoolroom backed on to the lower moorland of Trannack Downs and it was here that the men heated water in an iron boiler which stood on a "brandiss" (an iron triangular frame on three legs) and under which was lit a fire of mainly wood, furze sticks and a little coal.

The water was brought in churns and was needed for tea-making and washing-up. The chapel had neither water nor electricity and it was not until the late 1930's that an earth toilet was built together with a small car park on the moor. Hitherto anyone in desperate need had to hop over a nearby hedge or call on Mrs Phillips in the only house near the chapel.

The two services on Sundays have followed the Methodist pattern since the 19th century with the singing of hymns accompanied on a foot-pedal pumped harmonium or American organ The sight of the lady organist pedalling furiously away, playing the keyboard and at the same time singing vigorously was for many boys the highlight of the service. Not so the sermon or the prayers which were often extempore and sometimes interminable though the were enlivened by the occasional swear-word introduced by one preacher in particular, one John Willy Thomas of Tregeseal, who became so carried away by his flowing prose that he quite forgot where he was!

Fortunately, many children were excused the chapel services but Sunday School was virtually as obligatory as weekday schooling irrespective of whether their parents attended chapel or not.

Tregerest with its large schoolroom attracted many from down nearer the village partly, perhaps, as an extension of weekday attendance with ones' peers, but also due to some friendly rivalry or less friendly friction among families or neighbours. Surprisingly though, even living in such an enclosed community there was very little of that, we all rubbed along together.

Sunday school also followed the hymn singing and prayer pattern, the latter often becoming off-the-cuff sermons, there would be a short address usually with a bible theme and bible reading and teaching lessons. For these we were split into small groups (boys and girls were separate at all times) and the girls and young boys were instructed by the older girls and women.

For the older boys this was the best part of the afternoon as they were "taught" by the men. The bible topic of the day would be swiftly dealt with and there would be a longer period recounting tales of the previous day's local sports or events, which, in winter, was mainly the day's fox or rabbit hunting!

Sunday School Anniversary

Following on from our Sunday school activities, arguably the most important day of the year for everyone, was the anniversary held in June. At Tregerest a suitable corner of a nearby field was made available and forms were taken out for the band (usually Pendeen Silver Band) and adults to sit on. In the early afternoon everyone, around 50 in all, dressed in"going to town" clothes would line up behind the band and, led by the Sunday School and "Band of Hope" banners, would march down to Newbridge and then back up the hill - almost 2 miles. In hot weather with the tar on the road bubbling and becoming sticky it was not at all popular with many children.

Then the games began, most popular being the egg and spoon, the three-legged, sack and straight races which followed but even more popular was the 'tea treat' 6 inch diameter saffron buns washed down with bottles of Eddy's "pop" which were sealed with a captive marble in the neck. Sharing the adults' tea with its jam and cream splits, saffron and other special cakes was relished, following which there would be a concert. The pay-off came on the following afternoon when all the pupils were encouraged to contribute to a special service and concert by the children. There was some singing and some readings but many performed poetry.

How's your best cow getting on?

The poems were largely of a pious nature, some of the "little angel" variety but occasionally there would be a humorous one such as that which told of the farmer who added water to his milk before selling it; not unknown in those days. One night some lads from that village put the pump on his well out of action and thereafter he would be greeted with cries of "how's your best cow getting on?" and "is she any better yet?"

All pupils at Tregerest were awarded an annual prize of a book. This would be chosen by those who could do so by visiting the celebrated stationers Messrs Saundry of Chapel Street, Penzance, who held a list of the value of book each pupil was allowed and could choose accordingly in readiness for the presentation.

Apart from the important festivals of Christmas and Easter, the other major festival which had most significance of all for country folk was the harvest festival, the hymns being sung with particular fervour.

Much of the fruit and some of the produce had to be bought and the quantity produced and displayed in front of the pulpit was quite amazing. On the following Monday night the school room at Tregerest would be filled to bursting for the auction sale of the produce in aid of chapel fund~ and caught up in the fun and competitiveness of the occasion many lots were sold at far more than their true value.

The Sunday School Anniversaries were almost the only times apart from the "Band of Hope" meetings and outings that chapels visited one another. Among the notables in the two chapels were the Oates family, the Williams, Harveys, Eddys, Jelberts, Grenfells, Bottrell, Richards and local miller and preacher Charlie Remphrey.

A final memory of these years were the outings with the "Band of Hope" and the Sunday School to places like St Ives and Carbis Bay when the men, many only in their twenties, turned out in their Sunday or second best suit as befitted a Chapel occasion. They were the salt of the earth!"

CHAPTER 8

NEWBRIDGE AREA

HIGHER BODINNAR
Harry and Marie Hosken

Harry and Marie Hosken with their children Stella age five and Desmond age three moved to the farm known as Higher Bodinnar near Newbridge in the Parish of Sancreed in 1946. From the time of their marriage in 1938, they farmed at Bosullow in the parish of Madron. The farmhouse at Higher Bodinnar needed updating and was without bath, indoor toilet and had no electricity.

The farm was of some 37 acres; mainly grassland and arable but included some moorland. During the nine years that Harry and Marie farmed there they milked a small herd of Guernsey cows reared their own young stock and grew crops such as potatoes, corn, cabbage and mangolds. They also kept a small flock of hens and some pigs.

Annually, Mr Willy Mann from Morvah would come with his tractor and threshing machine to thresh the corn, which was later milled at Carthew Farm in Newbridge owned by Mr Cecil Merrifield. Threshing day was very labour intensive and all the neighbouring farmers helped as the threshing machine progressed from farm to farm in the district.

Harry was not in favour of having a tractor so he worked the farm with two carthorses. When Desmond was old enough he was trained to drive them as well. During their time there a milking machine was installed

Stella and Desmond attended the local primary school at Newbridge (now long since closed), then both progressed to the grammar schools in Penzance. They travelled by bus and boarded it at the end of the lane in Newbridge hill. During the nine years at Higher Bodinnar the family worshipped at Tregerest Methodist Church where Harry became a Steward.

Marie was a founder member of Sancreed Women's Institute holding the office of both President and Secretary.

Thunderbolt

During their time at Higher Bodinner an incident, which was recorded in *'The Cornishman'*, could have resulted in a fatality.

One Sunday morning; the cows were being milked when there was a very severe electrical storm. A thunderbolt travelled up the farm lane, which measured a half of a mile, splitting telegraph poles as it progressed. Eventually it struck a milking machine bucket, which was being handled by Marie. The cows bellowed, one was struck down but not killed and Marie fell to the floor. Since it was summer time Marie was wearing sandals with crepe soles. Had she not been wearing these sandals she would surely have been killed and probably the cow as well.

Harry and Marie eventually gave up the farm in 1955 due to Harry's ill health. They became sub postmaster and sub postmistress at Heamoor in the Borough of Penzance from October 1955.

LOWER BODINNAR

William Bottrell, born Madron 1842, married Anna Parker North of Drift. They emigrated to the USA, where their daughter Ellen was born about 1872. They moved to Canada and there, in about 1875 John Charles was born. By 1877 William's health was failing so they decided to return home and he died soon after this, just before Richard Albert was born.

Ken Bottrell: "Great uncle, John Charles Bottrell, made his career as a carpenter at Drift. Grandfather, Richard Albert Bottrell, served his time at the blacksmiths shop at Buryas Bridge. He shod all the ponies at Geevor Mine for years, walking there and riding the skip down the mine where he shod the ponies all day then walked back home again in the evening. When he married he farmed at Tresvennack, Paul for about 13 years.

He bought Lower Bodinnar and went there to farm in 1919. There were four stones found near the river two each side. When tin streaming had taken place these stones were placed flat with a round hole in the middle holding an upright pole as a whim and, using a horse, raised tin ore When the hole on one side became worn the stone was turned over and there was a hole for working it on the other side. This whim would be used for primitive streaming and mining."

Mining (whim) stone, Ken Bottrell at Lower Bodinnar.

Ken Bottrell won many prizes with a pony. He said, "It was our Dartmoor pony 'Nigger'. Father bought him at Helston Plum Fair for £11 at 12 months old. My brother Claude rode him first. That pony would jump 4ft 6ins to 4ft 9ins and was only 12 hands (ie 4ft high"). So he was jumping more than his own height! A very versatile animal he was used by us to bank all the potatoes and scarify the kale."

Baleswidden Mine used to employ 1200 men. In the early days they took the tin ore to Penzance with a horse and cart. Instead of going straight to the port they would go to the Bog Inn, have a few pints, some got drunk, drive down through Hallantackan (Newbridge) , through the river, (no bridge there then), and on to Penzance. Bog Inn, a 'kiddleywink' licensed to sell only beer, developed such a reputation for the fights that took place there that it was closed. The last person who lived at Bog Inn was Walter Harry.

Jump boy and tell them I died a hero

Vaughen Oats of Newbridge worked at the china clay works near St Just. He would take his steam lorry loaded up with china clay from there to the port at Penzance. One day going down Newbridge hill, with his stoker with him, the brakes gave way. He said to his stoker *'Jump boy and tell them I died a hero!.'* Nothing happened to him!

There is a Harold Harvey painting of the Newbridge area. In that picture is a thatched cottage surrounded with roses. My mother, (who would be 93 now), remembered seeing the cottage, which has now been demolished, on her way to school. Receven Vean, which is also in the picture, was built in 1902. In the picture too is the threshing machine house."

Catchall Dairy Co. had this building erected in 1896/97 for use as a branch dairy. J Williams Snr. was in charge of it. In October 1901 Newbridge branch dairy was closed so the building was sold to the Threshing Machine Company in 1905.

(A likely kinsman of Ken Bottrell was William Bottrell of St Levan, author of *Legends and Hearthside Stories of West Cornwall.*)

The name Bottrell comes down from the Botreaux family of Botreaux Castle from which also Boscastle takes its name. The village of Boscastle was featured as Castle Boterel in Thomas Hardy's book *'A pair of blue eyes'.*

NEWBRIDGE

Village of Newbridge

Ron Prowse: "Whilst Sancreed Churchtown was the historical and spiritual centre of the parish, even though it was on the border with Madron parish, Newbridge became its commercial heart from the late 19th early 20th c. Some of the *village* houses and its mill were indeed in Madron parish, the river coming down from the northwest forming the boundary.

Newbridge owed its pre-eminence to the main road running through it from the mining areas of St Just and Pendeen to Penzance and it was money from the financiers of the enterprises there which paid for the rebuilding of the bridge over the river (downstream it becomes the Newlyn river) in 1843. It was deemed necessary to handle the increasing traffic to and from the mines. Later in the century two new chapels were built to replace the earlier meeting houses, one in the village and one at Tregerest a mile to the west.

By this time Newbridge boasted a shop; a store for coal and paraffin; (later petrol), 2 general hauliers, a major smithy housed in the 19thc drill hall, a carpenter wheelwright, an abbatoir/retail butcher, a public house and a post-office which delivered to most of the parish as well as parts of Madron, Morvah, and St Just parishes.

Newbridge School

Newbridge School was built in 1876 as a County Council "Board" school (i.e. run by an appointed board of appointed local worthies and replacing a village "dame" school) and it had over 100 pupils on the register in the 1880s but it is doubtful if all attended at any one time. By the 1920s and 30s the regular attendance was around 60 children aged from 5 to 14 years taught in just 2 classes.

Newbridge School 1936.

Back Row: Ross King, Billy Lawry, Howard Clemens, Cecil Trembath, Gwennie Grenfell, ? ?, Joe Martin, Russell Eddy, Russell Grey, Michael Ellis.
Middle Row: Leslie Oats, Ken Oates, Doreen Merrifield, Dolly Grenfell, Nora Olds, Jean Rowe, Myrtle Grenfell, Arnold Oats, Lennard Harvey, Cecil Merrifield.
Front Row: Ronnie Prowse, Francis Lanyon, Robert Lanyon, ? ?, Lawrence Lawrey, Donald Trewern, Clarence Olds.

To the north and east the stream was able to power 2 grist mills at Carthew and Roskennals. These served local farms by rough milling their threshed grain to render it edible as cattle and horse feed.

To the west the road climbed up Trig-the-wheel hill, well named from the practice of sliding a U~shaped iron shoe about 15ins long (a Trig) secured to the wagon frame by a chain under one of the wagon wheels to act as a downhill brake. To the south of this road rose Trannack Hill and Derval Downs, to the north the south facing slopes had been "broken-in" in earlier years resulting in 5 or 6 farms of about 30 - 35 acres each.. "

The New Bridge

In 1843 a new bridge was built in the village formerly called Hallentacken. The adoption of a plan drawn up by Mr. Edward Harvey of Penzance was proposed and seconded by John Paynter and Revd. M. N. Peters.

Balleswidden Mine subscribed (£5), John Thomas (£1), and Philip Marrack (£1) but more was needed. The advantage to the people of St Just, (particularly the mine adventurers), in having a wider, safer bridge across the Newlyn River was stressed so with this in mind the bridge was built.

From earlier times this road and the lanes around were busy with the activity of packhorse mules, carrying tin ore, making their way to the Penzance area.

From 1700 onwards it seems that almost all the tin ore from St Just and Pendeen area was being taken to Stablehobba or Chyandour for smelting, coinage and stamping. As time went on most of the copper ore was smelted out of the county in places like Swansea.

Coal was plentiful but coal deliveries from the quayside still had to pass through Newbridge and up over Dry Carn.

Steam traction engines were being used by 1899 at Levant Mine pulling 4 or 5 trucks of tin and copper ore. These trucks would be loaded with coal or wood for the return journey.

In November 1908 Mr Llewellyn, estate agent of Mr Robyns Bolitho, told the committee at the Western Hotel at Penzance, about Levant engines taking water and damaging fences at Tremayne, near Newbridge. It was suggested that a small acknowledgment should be paid by the mine so the tractions might take water in the future without trouble to either party. The local authorities were much concerned with excessive wear to the road caused by these machines. A committee of traction engine owners was set up with Captain Nicholas, manager, representing Levant.

In June 1909 he was instructed not only to try and obtain permission for their heavy engines to run, but to ask that they should be allowed heavier engines in the future. "It is doubtful whether these heavy engines do more damage than the smaller ones owing to there being not so much backslip with them." The heavier engines were also said to be more efficient owing to the stiff hills to be negotiated. The Highways Committee were bitterly opposed to the engine traffic, but ultimately a satisfactory solution was reached. Willie Alford tells of his 'Granfer Billie' driving his steam traction engine, pulling china clay to Penzance, and coal to Levant on the return journey. There were several steam engines working at the mines. From earliest times this road was subject to very heavy use and was costly to repair.

The St Just Road tollgate at Tremethick Cross

From the mid 1700s tollgates were introduced and fees levied by trusts, whose role it was to maintain the roads in their care. Revenues raised from these fees were used to fund the work of improving turnpike routes. Toll keepers were provided with a home and were on call twenty-four hours a day. They needed to be available to lift the toll barriers and collect the fee. Close to a crossroads these toll keepers were entrusted with the job of controlling all traffic.

On the St Just road from Penzance at Tremethick Cross a tollgate was erected in a prominent position from 1863. One wonders why, when most were about to be abolished? Possibly it was because of the heavy traffic with china clay, tin and coal. Now a private residence, the tollhouse and the gatekeeper's porch are still there on this busy road. (This was a route much used by Sancreed folk).

Horses with their heavy loads, herds of cattle, sheep and pigs on the way to market; and later increasingly vehicular traffic, all had to be paid for. Pedestrians paid no toll at all. By 1885 all tollgates were abolished and the council managed the roads.

Newbridge Chapel

Until recently there had been a Methodist Society worshipping in Newbridge since the early 1830s. People used to worship in the old carpenter's shop, later used as a paint shop by a local garage, now a private garage/workshop currently owned by a local resident.

The first Chapel on the site of the recently closed Chapel was thought to have been a converted outhouse, mentioned as The Wesleyan Chapel and Premises in a document dated 1849.

Mrs Rowe, Postmistress, presentation on retirement, at Newbridge Chapel.

In 1854 a new building was erected for public worship - described as "barn type". Dimensions: 28 feet long by 21 feet wide and 12 feet high to accommodate around 100 people. The present building is mentioned in the Cornish Telegraph Thurs 4th August 1892 - an account of the stone laying.

Plans were shown which included a schoolroom and a Chapel, at a projected cost of £500.

The Sunday School Banner bought c1920 is now in the St Just Methodist Church. It was used at Sunday school parades and was restored in 1990 by Mrs. Irene Carter. The restored banner was unfurled at a special service led by Rev. Philip D Williams on 1st March 1991. The cost of renovation was £200. Banner reads: 'Newbridge Wesleyan Sunday School Established 1935', on 2 scrolls above and below a picture of Jesus carrying a lamb, among several sheep on a rocky road (hand-painted).

Newbridge Chapel closed in December 2005 after the Carol Service.

THE STORY OF THE REYNOLDS PLOUGHS

Barrie Reynolds: "William Giles Reynolds started as a Newbridge blacksmith in premises over the bridge in Madron parish. By about 1908 he moved to a new building in Bodinnar Lane, Newbridge, Sancreed. In the 1930s the Drill Hall was purchased and it became the new blacksmiths shop and the former premises were converted into a dwelling house for the Reynolds family.

Previously William Giles Reynolds had served his time in Devonport Dockyard. In the late 1930s he was still there as blacksmith but his son William Herbert was working separately and described by Kellys as Implement maker; which business was later carried on by his two sons, Frank and Jack.

The Reynolds firm existed at Newbridge for a hundred years, up until 1968 and they are believed to be the first blacksmiths to start in business in Newbridge. In the early days fifteen men used to work in the blacksmith's shop, serving a five-year apprenticeship. Among these was Jim Williams. Rev. Philip Williams worked at the forge for a time as a boy, having to stand on a box to reach his work, hence the Reynolds told a story that they had given him his first lift-up in life; Phil's mother used to send him to work with gingerbread sandwiches which he swapped with his friends."

Jim Williams of St Just: "In January 1936 I started an apprenticeship with W H Reynolds and Sons, Agricultural Blacksmiths and Farriers. Wages were 2/6 per week; the hours were 8am until 5.30pm. This was a five year apprenticeship with one year as an 'improver'. Mr Reynolds and his two sons worked in the shop, which was an old drill hall. There were two forges with large leather bellows, a portable forge, a twist drill, and a big shears that came from Levant Mine. Worked by a 30cwt cast iron wheel, to cut ¼" plate and punch holes for harrow tines. It needed two men to turn it. No electricity in those days or oxy acetylene welding. All iron to be hand forged in best Crown and Thistle, good workable iron. The coal used was Welsh steam shipped in via Portreath.

In 1936 before the advent of tractors, horses worked the farms, so we shod an average of 20 horses per day. The first job in the morning was to make 10 pairs of shoes. The farmer would ride the horses to the shop, jump on a bus, and go to Penzance Market and pick the horse up on the way home.

We made the majority of horse-drawn implements which were used on the farm, roller frames, chain harrows, ploughs, cultivators, cast axles, iron work for carts and field gates.

A double plough took five and a half days to make and a tine harrow took three days.

Wooden wheels were made by Tommy Grenfell in the adjoining carpenter's shop and we fitted the binds.

When war came, the farmers had to plough more land for potatoes to feed the people. This is when the Reynolds 'two and four furrow plough' was developed. About that time the tractor made its first appearance. Cornwall War Agricultural Committee obtained tractors to plough more land for increased food production. These were trailer ploughs and not hydraulic as we have today.

In 1949, I left and started my own business and bought the blacksmiths shop at Kelynack."

"The old firm of Reynolds and Sons, Agricultural Merchants, continues to assist Lord Woolton in his "Eat more Potatoes" appeal. If you chanced to call in at the works during the past week you would have seen a magnificent array of some twelve four-furrow potato ploughs for different parts of the county; and also other large implements, which is a high record for full production for a small village "The Cornishman, 4th February 1943."

Barrie Reynolds: "They used to start work at 8 am. At 10am my gran used come out with a basketful of crowst. Everybody, even the customers who were perhaps having a horse shod, would pick up a horseshoe nail box and sit on it. Out would come two big jugfuls of tea and they would have a sandwich or a pasty or something.

On the wall is a photo of a gate made for Trevaylor. All the scrollwork was done by hand.

The people who owned Trevaylor, Brooke Bond Tea, wanted gates there that were like the gates of Buckingham Palace, and that was what we made for them. All the light parts were painted in gold leaf paint. They are still there."

Keith & Jennifer Eddy.

The Fountain Inn, Newbridge.

Newbridge Garage

Keith Eddy: "Before we came Mrs Earl, (who was landlady of the Fountain Inn), ran the filling station and had a little shop here. There was no garage, no repairs. I began my career agricultural engineering with W.T.Teagle, and at 26, I started this rural garage serving the farming community in 1967. All round here were dairy farmers producing milk. We repaired cars and did some work for agriculture including tractors, and also lorries for Vivian Cock. There were four of us working here, two young boys, another chap and myself. My wife Jennifer was the secretary.

This place was owned by Frank and Vicky Jelbert of Tremaine Farm.

There was a little cow's house behind the garage when I came here. Mr and Mrs Bennett used to milk six cows, and where the pumps are was a cottage. We have been here 42 years and have loved the life."

RECEVEN

Phyllis Jilbert

This house, Receven Vean, was built in 1902. It has two wells, one of which the village people used the other was for the house.

"I married Thornton Jilbert in 1951 and we came here to farm on 25 acres. We used to rear turkeys, ducks and chicken for Christmas. One year we plucked 100 birds. It meant staying up nearly all night.

The Co-op took all those that were not ordered by private customers. They were displayed in the shop window. I wish I had gone and taken a picture of them. After all that work my fingers were sore. I said I'd never do it again; never go back to those days. Then Thornton got a part time job as a postman because the farm wasn't paying. He used to get out of bed 4am to milk the cows before he went on his post round. (see Sellan)

The old Recevean farmhouse nearby, dates back a few hundred years. It has been suggested that it was the only house around here at one time, surrounded by rough land. When it was being restored many pieces of millstone were found which suggests there may have been a mill there at some time".

LITTLE RECEVEN
Dr Dyke and his early motor cars

The Olds were butchers at Little Receven from 1904 for about 50 years. First Charles, then Charles B. Olds and his large family. At Little Receven the killing shop is still there almost unchanged.

Little Receven was a Riding School in the early 1970s and was bought by Dr. Dyke in 1979. He formerly had a surgery in Penzance. His hobby is restoring and driving early motors cars of which he has about six. The following two he drives regularly.

White Steam Car Model L. 20 hp. 1908. This car was produced in Cleveland, Ohio, USA and imported in 1908 by the White Sewing Machine Co in London It has a 7 seat body. A William Garton of Southampton was the first owner who used it until 1915. The body was removed and the chassis went to war service in France.

Dr Dyke purchased the car in 1988 and restored it to full working order for the first time since 1915. After that it has covered about 10,000 miles across Europe. The 20hp compound engine accelerates well but is limited by the gearing to 40mph. The 2-speed gearbox in the rear axle and condenser at the front gives about 50 miles per fill of water. A mixture of 80% petrol to 20% diesel will return about 6 to 8 mpg locally!

White Surrey Made in 1902. It is the only one known to exist. The Surrey, with its three-seater configuration (with the servant-man seated outside at the back), was originally owned by Sir Charles Ross who had a smallholding in Scotland of 356,600 acres! He lived in Banglow Castle, which is now owned by Mr Al Fayed. Sir Charles ran it for 4 or 5 years and then it was laid up. It was pushed on its side in the coach house. When Sir

Charles died his third wife married the Count Develin. He, with the gardener, tried to steal it in the late forties early fifties. It never really worked. It was sold from Banglow Castle in 1968 to a motor dealer in Glasgow.

Dr. Dyke: "I bought it in 1993 and restored it for the 1996 London to Brighton centenary race. I have raced in four 'London to Brightons' now. I also smashed it up in 2002. It was restored on Salvage Squad and shown for an hour on that TV programme."

BOSVENNING

Arnold Oates

"I was born at Jericho Farm, Newbridge on December 11th 1926. I cannot remember how old I was when we left for Bosvenning Farm, Newbridge, just a toddler.

The only remembrance of Jericho, was collecting a whole conger at the top of the lane, left by the fishmonger. I held on to mother's hand tightly, being so afraid of it.

From an early age I was always singing, no doubt handed down. Father had a good bass voice; mother's was a fine contralto. These were natural voices.

I sang my first solo on my third birthday; this was at Brane Chapel December 1929. I cannot remember singing, but

Leslie, Arnold, Athelstan and Mrs Oates

Athelstans brother, Wilfred a well known Newbridge cattle dealer.

walking back to the pew, a lady by the name of Mrs. Waters handed me a packet of sweets. When I sat down mother who was playing the organ and facing the congregation, gave me a terribly black look, which meant not to eat sweets in chapel.

Bless This House

An invitation came from Tregavarah Chapel who were giving a concert on a particular Saturday evening with a special request that I would sing.

Having to practise while my pals were out playing did not go down very well, so I was adamant that I was not going to sing. Mum and Dad begged me, bribed me, tried all ways to change my mind, but I still said no.

After a while, I felt as if I was being very stubborn, so suggested a compromise. I would sing if Leslie sang. He was my elder brother by nearly four years. I felt as if I was on a good wicket as he never sang but with some persuasion they got him to sing. The evening came; he sang "Bless this House". The concert ended and then the usual refreshments came. We boys certainly knew how to eat.

Sometime after 10pm, when we had arrived home and gone to bed, the air raid siren sounded and we two lads leaned out of the bedroom window, to watch the searchlights, and heard the drone of aircraft and crackle of gunfire.

Suddenly there was a blinding flash followed a few seconds later by a loud explosion.

Going to the morning service next day we were told that Tregavarah Chapel received a direct hit by a landmine reducing it to rubble.

**I couldn't resist reminding my brother that "lots of good came out of your solo",
"Bless this house, dear Lord we pray. Keep it safe by night and day."
Then it was blown up three hours later! This was Leslie's first and last solo.**

A fair cop

During the summer evenings the youngsters of the village congregated at the village square, riding their bicycles.

One such evening looking towards Ropers Corner, we noticed our community policeman, P.C. Kersey pushing his bicycle. He was a fair copper. Many times he caught us riding without lights. "Walk home boys, no riding without lights". We daren't ride; we knew he would lurk in some by lane.

We had great respect for him, so much so by the time he reached the village, the puncture outfit was ready, one lad called at a house for dessert spoons, to use as tyre lifters. The bicycle was turned upside down, tyre off, tube out, puncture mended, tube in, tyre on, blown up.

All this time P.C. Kersey was leaning against the wall, calmly watching. I think he got a buzz. "Thank you boys", he said, "that saves me a long walk to Pendeen".

At the age of fifteen I joined the Heamoor Male Voice Choir and later became of a member of the St Just Operatic Society, as well as a member and soloist for a number of years with the Penzance Choral Society and the Truro Kenwyn Barber Gilbert and Sullivan Singers.

From the age of eighteen I was a pupil of Madame Gladys Harries of Kingsbridge, who herself was a protégé of the world famous contralto, Dame Clara Butt.

In the early years choral singing in churches and chapels was very strong. As oratorio was my favourite, demand was great. "The Messiah, Elijah, Creation, Judas Maccabeaus" and many other works which took me as guest artist as far away as Buckfastleigh, Tiverton, Plymouth, Torquay, Bristol, and of course the Isles of Scilly.

The most demanding time was Easter. Passion Sunday, Palm Sunday, Good Friday and Easter Day: engagements for this period were booked three years in advance. Some of the most important people, who never receive the accolade which they deserve, are the accompanists.

At times you have a full orchestra, but in the main you relied on the good folk who were quite willing to accompany a singer, not only for performances, but the many hours of rehearsal that it entails. It is a pity that young fellows are not joining male voice choirs nowadays but good accompanists are equally as scarce.

Two local ladies from St.Just, Ethel Angwin and Mary Treglown both accompanists are still active and have been for many more years than we wish to remember. Without such dedicated people, vocal and choral works would cease to be performed.

Time of course goes on and at the age of 51 my singing took a terrible blow with the onset of a breathing problem and this affected my performance. I decided my solo work had ended. Disappointing but it was a wise decision.

However, the Cornwall Police Male Voice Choir was looking for a Musical Director after the passing of Edgar Kessell. Edward Goldsmith had filled the post for one season.

Following on from the well known Edgar Kessell was daunting but I took up the challenge.

During a period of 20 years I directed 498 concerts with countless rehearsals. It was a tremendous experience and a thrill also to conduct on several occasions for the Massed Police Choir, the Devon and Cornwall Police Band and the Stan Hackett Concert Band of 55 players from Exeter.

Now at my age, I am able to reminisce about those days and my love of music.

I worked for Simpsons, the local outfitters for in Penzance for 20 years and managed their Truro branch for 21 years. Now in my 81st year I try to keep active with a number of hobbies and interests."

Note: In August 1941 bombs were dropped at Bosvenning and Roskennels Farm, Newbridge. Three exploded one did not.

BOSVENNING

Lady Penzance the mare of Sancreed!!

J.H.Care: "St Buryan races were held on Easter Monday at Boskenna Home Farm. That Easter Sunday morning this Irish horse and jockey were trying out the racecourse. My father ordered them off the ground."

This horse was in fact going to try to beat the famous mare 'Lady Penzance', which was owned by Mr. John Rowe from Bosvenning, Newbridge and was ridden by his son Johnnie Rowe.

In fact that gentleman's horse never did beat the mare 'Lady Penzance'. He came unstuck in the 'box jump'.

Betty Grey: "John Rowe (1850 – 1912) was a farmer at Bosvenning Farm Sancreed. However his great love was racehorses – which he imported from Ireland and raced in the southwest. His son Johnnie beacame a well known jockey and rode many of these horses. One, called 'Lady Penzance', was exceptional and it was with her that Johnnie became famous as a jockey from Bristol to Penzance, in the Bristol and West races.

Sadly one day there was an accident in which 'Lady Penzance' fell, partly landing on Johnnie. This resulted in lung damage, from which he died in October 1906 at the age of 22 years. It was the largest funeral in the district for many years. There were over one hundred carriages in the procession. Many mourners were unable to obtain admittance to the church at Sancreed.

After this tragedy – heartbroken – John Rowe gave 'Lady Penzance' to Major Bolitho on the condition that she should not race again. So 'Lady Penzance' ended her days being well cared for at the Bolitho estates at Ponsandane.

Tragedy struck again when three months later when Susanna Rowe, his wife, died, (some say of grief).

Their daughter Millie was by this time attending 'Miss Bell's school for young ladies' at Alverton. She would drive herself to school in her pony and trap, which was stabled at the then, Western Hotel.

Millie grew up to meet and marry Arthur Paull Glanville, who, after the First World War had joined the Hong Kong Government." **Betty Grey (their daughter)**

Bosvenning – Town Place

Originally a manor, Bosvenning was known in earlier times as Bosvennen.

From 1850 until 1912 it was farmed by John Rowe but Frank Newton took over the tenancy, paying an annual rent of £133 until 1919.

In April 1919, Charles Hattam from St Just followed his elder brother, Henry Hattam (see Botrea) to Sancreed parish. Charles purchased Bosvenning from Viscount Clifden, of the Lanhydrock Estate, for £4100. It consisted of 94 acres, 2 roods and 16 perches. Later, Charles' brother William and their mother, Elizabeth nee Thomas, also moved to Bosvenning.

Charles, who had previously run a milk round in St Just but came from a farming family, married Minnie Johns of Treeve. Tragically, he died in 1922 after falling off a cart returning from Penzance and ownership of the farm was then split between his two young sons, Charles Henry aged just 14 and William John aged just 7 years. There was also a daughter, Elizabeth Hilda, who moved to Brea after marrying Herbert Williams. Their uncle, William Hattam, died just two years later in 1924.

Charles Henry did not marry but William John (known as Jack) married Mabel Nicholls from Higher Drift, daughter of Samuel Nicholls. They had three sons, Roger, Michael and Graham.

Graham Hattam still lives in Newbridge with his wife Barbara, having farmed Bosvenning until he retired. Roger eventually came out of farming and Michael moved on to farm Jericho, also in Sancreed parish.

Bosvenning - the James' with Barbara Hattam.

ROSKENNALS MILL

History from 1695

A fascinating restored water mill now stands in about three and a half acres bordered by a stream. Fortunately the history of the mill has been well documented.

The first reference to Roskennals Mill is in 1695 when it appeared on a survey map of the Earl of Radnor's estates. A lease was granted in 1725 to Melchisedeck Baynard comprising the watercourses, pools and leats with the Earl retaining the right to cut trees, to hawk and to hunt. Ten years later Humphrey Roberts of Ludgvan took the lease at a rent of £7 pa.

At some point between 1751 and 1767 the mill passed to George Hunt of Lanhydrock Estate and in 1784 the lease was taken by John Hoskins with the hawking, hunting, fishing and fowling rights reserved to the landlord.

An advertisement appeared in the West Briton of August 8th 1828 offering the mill to let by tender and again a tenant was sought via the Royal Cornwall Gazette in 1854.

In 1932 the main driving wheel of the mill was cast at Holman Bros. Foundry at Tregeseal. Cogs were made and fixed by T. Grenfell, the village carpenter. From 1930 onwards there was no one in the district to dress the stones so this was done by the miller James Newton.

In 1946 the mill was leased to W.C. Remphrey who later purchased it. He was a nephew of Mrs. Newton who bought it from Thomas Trevor Giles of Kemyel for £1,000 in 1953.

In 1964 milling of corn ceased at Roskennals Mill after nearly 300 years. W.C.Remphrey (Charlie) had been the miller there for 28 years, sold it to John Charlton who, with his daughter Ruth, completely restored the wheel using oak for the spokes.

Ella & Gerry Plumb, (the latter a well known artist), purchased Roskennals Mill in 1997. Major work was done on the mill building, machinery was removed to the ground floor and the building was given a new roof.

It was then converted into living accommodation keeping as much of the character as was feasible.

Both the mill and the granary are Grade II listed and were sold again in 2007 to

Matthew and Verity Hill. Their aim is to ensure the mill and other buildings are protected and maintained for future generations

NEWBRIDGE SHOW AND SPORTS

Founded 1932.   Affiliated to B.S.J.A.

President : J. H. PROWSE, Esq.

PROGRAMME of

LIGHT HORSES, TROTTING, HURDLE JUMPING, DONKEY RACING, RIDING and EXPRESS LETTER RACES

Exhibition Driving by M. L. Oats, Esq.

Demonstration : England's No. 1 Dog " Tearaway Tim "

FRIDAY, AUGUST 10th, 1973, at 12 noon.

To be held at **NEWBRIDGE**

By kind permission of
J. C. Jelbert, Esq., Boswednan Farm, Newbridge.

Judges : JUMPING: R. E. Roberts, Esq.
LIGHT HORSES and GYMKHANA : Mr. & Mrs. W. Dennis.

Timekeeper : R. Clifton, Esq.

Course Builder : C. Bottrell, Esq.

All Entries to be taken on the Field.

Amplification : Dobbs' Amplifiers, Pz.

LICENSED BAR and CATERING by Mrs. J. Hammett, Newbridge.
(Licensed hours, 2 to 8 p.m.).

Admission : Car & Driver 30p.   Adults 15p.
Children 5p.

Hon. Secretary :
C. B. Olds, Esq., ' Boslow,' 4 Penalverne Drive, Penzance

PROGRAMME PRICE 5p

Lucky Nos. : 1st Prize £1.   2nd Prize 50p.

CHAPTER 9

SELLAN AREA

GREAT SELLAN FARM

Phyllis Jilbert and her brother Norman Hosking tell of growing up at Sellan
Three children die in 20 days

Phyllis Jilbert: "James Henry Hosking 1st, (1854-1913) my grandfather, was a champion ploughman and his great grandson James Hosking still has the plough. He moved to Great Sellan in 1893 from Tresvennack in Paul. The following year 1894 he and his wife Mary, nee Gwennap, lost three children with diphtheria in 20 days. He was left with three boys. The infected children had been looked after in a building away from the farmhouse.

There were pig houses outside near the back of the house and the children's father was so upset that he pulled them all down.

In August 1899 fire burnt three of his hayricks in the mowhay. He helped to keep the other ricks and buildings from burning by throwing water over them till the fire engine arrived from Penzance. This was delayed an hour and a half for want of horses to bring it. Then they had an accident on the way, coming in haste they injured a man and horse. Water was pumped from the river about 300 yards away which put the fire out.

Later his eldest son James Henry 2nd farmed at Bodellan in St Levan. His second son Edwin lived at Bodmin, and his youngest son Norman, my father, farmed Great Sellan. When my father died in 1928 aged 34, my mother Isabel had help from her father, John Lawry, and her brother to run the farm. The farm was a little distance from the house.

My brothers used to milk cows before they went to school. We all walked a mile home from Sancreed to dinner. Our teacher, Miss Bailey rode a bike from Penzance every day. Her sister used to teach us music. She taught me to play the piano.

No time for reading

I remember the evacuees coming. We attended school in the mornings and they went in the afternoons. We did not have room to accommodate any. There were 9 in our house 7 children, mother, and Granfer John Lawry who came to live with us when father died. We had no time to play in those days. We did not have homework but I had to wash the dishes for nine of us, which seemed to take me all evening.

When the library came my teacher sent home a library book. My mother said, "You take that back and tell the teacher you've no time for reading, you've got to work in the evenings."

I remember when I was 13 I used to iron 17 shirts on a Monday night. On leaving school I had to milk the cows and wash these ten-gallon milk churns. In those days a windmill (wind pump) was used to pump the water for Great Sellan Farm.

Father loved golfing and won many cups and trophies. He did not like farming. In 1919 he had the first motorbike in Sancreed.

Threshing Days

After Warwick Hosking retired his brother Leonard used to come to thresh our corn. It took three days. Two days on the golf course and one day at the farm. We would run home from school and go up in the barn to see all the corn. The men would try to put us in the corn bag! As I got older I would help mother carry up crowst for them, (about a dozen of our neighbouring farmers) and then help prepare their dinner.

We used to like to go down to Porthcurno to stay with Uncle James Henry (2nd) for our holidays. We thought that place was foreign!

Sometimes Uncle Edwin came down from Bodmin. At Easter he would send down Easter eggs when we were small.

Down a rocky lane below us, near where the reservoir is now, was an isolated cottage, and during the war in this cottage lived a conscientious objector, and with him a Czechoslovakian refugee doctor and his family.

We did not go far during the war. We went to the dance on Saturday nights in the village hall and whist drives once a week."

Phyllis's brother - Norman Hosking

"My grandfather James Henry Hosking died before I was born. He was a big man with a beard, well known for his hard work and a good ploughman. I heard he threw a man out of St Buryan pub once by his beard. He was asked by the landlord to come to Sellan from Tresvennack in Paul, to erect hedges, cultivate the moorland and improve the farm, which was about one hundred and forty acres, reckoned to be a pretty big farm at that time in Sancreed! It must have been in the 1890s and it seems he employed a few men to help by the accounts I have seen, as he made payments to over twenty men on some days when removing banks, filling pits and building hedges. He farmed Sellan for a few years and then sub-let half the acreage to the Penzance Golf Club, for Golf links. It was agreed for him and his sons to keep sheep there. This land was on the western side of the farm and a Mr Lane, the professional, lived near the southern end. The pavilion and his club house was at the other must it have been almost half a mile away.

I was born one year after the Great War, at Great Sellan Farm in a semi-detached cottage by the farmyard. In the other lived my grandfather and grandmother. My other grandmother lived about one hundred yards down the road in a farmhouse. I was the

Sellan Farm 1932.
Hosking family: Norman at top,
Mary, Phyllis, Jack, Arnold in front.

second in a family of seven, five boys and two girls. We lived in the cottage until I was six.

I remember a special occasion when I was taken in my fathers Morgan, a three-wheeler car to Ding Dong, (to see a donkey) but really to fetch Mrs Symons the midwife, to attend mother at her latest confinement.

Tradesmen call

We had several tradesmen callers in our schooldays 1920 - 1935. The butcher Rogers Bros with his pony and trap lived at Grumbla at one time, the baker was Harvey from St Just with pony and covered trap, the fish fellow from Newlyn with pony and trap shouting his wares, Ned Jenkin with the paraffin and candles etc. with pony and trap from a smallholding at Grumbla. Harry Waters came on bike and took orders for groceries on Tuesdays, delivered on Thursday by lorry. Tobias Symons and his van came with groceries on Monday. There was a man with needles and cottons and the French onion man with his bike and Dungey with leather bootlaces and his mouth organ at Christmas. Thomas Henry would walk in and stand up, he was given a copper or two and would go on his way again. I think he was one of the Levant mine survivors.

Then there were the gypsies - the James had their camp nearby in a lane by our field we called Claypits. They had a big tent and a lovely caravan. On Sunday mornings after father had been hunting rabbits on Saturday, one of us would run down to their camp with the rabbit skins for which we would get two pence each. Others in the district came with scrubbing brushes, clothes pegs, mats and other household things.

Then there were the Indians who came with a big case full of fancy things; brooches, hankies etc. and they were likely to go away cursing if you did not buy.

Norman - Horseman at 14!

After leaving school at 14, it was mainly work. My first job in the morning was to take the milk to Catchall Dairy. This meant bringing in the pony, brushing her and harnessing her, hitching her in the spring trap, then loading the milk churns and set off, about three miles around the road from Sellan. By the time I got back and tipped the skim milk in the barrel for the pigs, unhitched and put the pony in the stable, it was crowst time.

In winter the horses in the stable had to be fed, watered, groomed and the stable cleaned out before breakfast. At one time we had five horses, four big shires and the cob (pony). The year was then filled in with ploughing, sowing and harvesting. Wintertime calves and yearlings had to be fed; cows were kept in the sheds by night from about the end of November to the end of March. About twenty to thirty were fed with rolled corn, bran, flake maize etc. hay, turnips and mangolds. Straw was used if it was good and hay was in short supply. They were fed and milked before breakfast. The sheds had to be cleaned and the manure put into a heap in the rough yard and then the same to be loaded into carts and hauled to the appropriate fields. This was spread with an eval (fork) by hand. Saturday's job was to put corn into bags and take it to Roskennals Mill with horse and cart and bring back that which was taken the week before. If there was a space, to bring some bran, flake maize or sharps for the pigs. On Saturdays, mangolds were taken to the golf links for the sheep. Hay had to be taken out of the rick and carried into the shed every two or three days. This was mainly the routine of winter work.

In the Spring - Any land not ploughed in winter was done. The ground worked out and corn and grass seed sown. Cows were turned out by night (what a relief) and the sheep, then lambing were brought in from the golf links and looked after in closer fields. About half an acre of early potatoes and the same of late potatoes were planted. Putting potatoes to shoot (ie sprout) was a winter evening job by candlelight. Some fertiliser was sown on grass by hand from the trap.

Lime was delivered in lump by lorry. It was loaded into carts and put onto the field in small piles to quench and be spread with a shovel.

Summer - The early potatoes were lifted, the mangolds and turnips were hoed, the hay saved and the corn harvested. When we cut the corn I rode or led the cob as the third horse in the binder in the 'hilly' fields. Two horses drew the binder in the level fields. We then put the sheaves into shocks, and if the weather was catchy, these were put into mows

When the corn was ready, we took the sheaves (using two wagons) to be built into ricks, four to five acres in a rick for a half days threshing, depending on the crop. Then the mangolds had to be lopped and sorted, all this work so far I liked but I did not care for milking. Sheep were kept on the golf links, which was about half a mile from the farm. These had to be checked every day and Sunday mornings they were put in the fold to be tended, tails clipped, feet trimmed and rot checked for.

Pleasure: We played cricket or wrestled, climbed trees or just rode on our bikes. My older brother played cricket for the Sancreed team on Saturday afternoons and asked the younger brothers to give him practice beforehand.

I went to town on Saturday evenings to the pictures with some mates. Penzance, The Terrace and Market Jew Street would be full of young people, in the evening. Many of the shop girls would trip up and down the street after leaving work about 8 o'clock and this was where they met young men.

On Sunday evenings the promenade would be crowded with people, parading up and down or listening to Penzance Silver Band, and the Salvation Army playing and singing.

My brother had a motorbike, which he sold and we pooled our money and bought a car, a twelve-horse power Wolsey Hornet saloon. The key was always left in the ignition and doors unlocked - no one locked doors or removed keys.

The car was taken to the blacksmith who made a hitch for it to tow a trailer and we started taking the milk to Catchall Factory with it and lambs to Truro market.

In these days before the war cars were becoming popular and even working people could save up and buy a new car or motorcycle. The cheapest car was one hundred pounds for a Ford eight.

Things seemed to go on very well for a couple of years, and then came the war. Young people over 18 were called up for the forces.

Farmers had orders to plough a lot of extra land to produce food for people and animals. I had word that I had passed for the army and received forms for deferment as I was working on the farm. Most males, who were able, joined the Home Guard. For a while things went on almost as normal.

My brother ordered a new tractor and a second hand Case tractor on spade lugs was sent to the farm for us to use while waiting for the new one. During the war in the spring of 1940, two part time workmen and I had been on the Golf Links, (which was part of the farm we had to plough) removing, levelling and filling in the bunkers with a horse and cart, picks and shovels.

After years of being a golf course for which my grandfather's farm hedges were torn down and the stone and earth used to make the greens and bunkers, once more we were bringing it back to farmland. I ploughed it with horses but soon we had the new Fordson tractor, plough and disc, tine harrows plus the big roller that had been used on the golf course. It was planted in corn the first year but the corn did not give much of a crop.

The second year it improved and six corn ricks were lined up for three days threshing. During the war years my brothers and I worked long hours and since we had a new tractor binder we cut some corn for neighbours."

Norman Hosking saw many changes in farming methods from threshing using a portable steam engine pulled by horses from farm to farm, to a steam traction engine and then the machine worked by a tractor to finally the combine harvester, which carried out the whole operation in one go.

Six cows killed

Their niece Sandra: "In the late sixties my father, James Henry 3rd, went to round up the Guernsey cows one morning and bring them in for milking when he came in and said that half a dozen of them were dead. They were sheltering under a hedge when lightning came down a telegraph pole and killed them.

We had some Italian prisoners of war on the farm modernising the cows' houses, the stalls and the 'parlour' floor. Gran was friendly towards them and one of them melted down a silver sixpence and made it into a little ring for her. She kept in touch with him for many years. Granny told us that her own mother died at the age of 18 of sunstroke. She was found dead at home."

Dead Man's Grave

James Hosking: "On the bend in the road over the hedge from the Golf Links stood a tree on a green known as Dead Man's Grave. It was here, it was said, a man was hanged long ago for stealing loaves of bread and this was at a time when food was very scarce".

GOLF LINKS

Penzance Golf Club

The Penzance Golf Club was opened at Sellan, Sancreed on the St Just bus route 3 ½ miles from Penzance in 1908. It was known as Golf Links, a surprising name for a club three miles from the sea! *(Fees – Gentlemen 2/- per day, 7/6 per week, 20/- per month. Ladies fees slightly reduced. No Play Sundays)*

The course, which was designed by Fred Whiting, the professional to the Royal St George's Club at Sandwich, was formally opened for play on New Year's Day 1909.

1923 Penzance guide

Golf: *The Penzance Links, a very interesting and sporting 18-hole course, are about 2 1/2 miles out of the town in Sancreed parish, and are beautifully situated. Standing on very high ground that quickly dries, a glorious view of the Bay and all the surrounding country can be obtained from any portion of the links. The altitude makes casual water through the green exceptional, even in the most rainy season, and a few grazing sheep, supplemented by ample mowing machinery, keep fairways and rough well under. Great attention has been given to the putting greens.*

The Links are very accessible, the G.W.R. motor¬cars to Pendeen pass the Pavilion three times a day on the outward journey, and twice in the afternoon on the return journey.

Willie Lane - golfer

From 1897 Willie Lane of Mullion learned the skills of golf club making and green keeping from his father who was the club professional there. On the first day of 1910 he asked his father to release him from his job at Mullion to take the post of professional instructor and steward at the Penzance Golf Club at Sancreed. He had just got married and told his father that a 25/- a week wage and a bungalow at Sancreed were better than the 17/- a week as understudy at Mullion. After moving to Sancreed he gave up his hobby of bass singing and set to work to extend the Penzance course from 9 to 18 holes. He stayed at the course for 30 years. His grand daughter, Margaret, has golf clubs he had made in her possession. They were made by hand in those days. In 1911 his only son Cyril was born.

Edith Try, nee Oats: "We knew the Lanes very well; they lived and worked on the Golf Links. I used to go up there for tea."

Remarkable Golf at Sancreed   *Cornish Evening Tidings 1932*

"Mr Cyril Lane, 21 year old son of Mr Willie Lane, the pro, at the Sancreed Golf Links, played a remarkable game of golf there last night. Starting at 11.30pm, he went round

in the dark in 77, and five long putts only failed to hole by half an inch. He was accompanied by a caddie with a hurricane lamp, which was the only light allowed except that when on the green, he was allowed to have a flash lamp in the hole. This was Mr Lane's first attempt and his score was, therefore more remarkable. An effort will be made to repeat it at an early date".

Professional Golfer.

Cyril went up and played at Wentworth in a competition

and won not having played there before or having previously seen the course. The prize money was only £5!

His father recalled with pride Cyril's achievement, at the age of 17 years, that in a professional golfers alliance at Lelant he holed in one at the first hole, two at the second hole and three at the third hole.

Cyril Lane was well known in West of England in the pre-war days. Like his father he played off scratch, and among his many holes in one was a distance of 292 yards.

Three American visiting golfers were expanding on their achievements. Cyril said to his caddy, "Lie on the ground and put the tee between your teeth". Cyril teed off with his club from the tee in the caddy's teeth. The Americans were dumbfounded.

Club House Fire - Willie Lane remembers

Recalling the clubhouse fire of May 19, 1938: "I made a set of clubs for Hartley Thomas of *'The Cornishman'*. We found a locker for them in the clubhouse but he never used them—the next day the place was burnt to the ground. The cause of the fire was never discovered."

Alfred Olds: "The Golf Links house was up by the road near Dead Man's Grave. In 1938 I was coming across the fields one morning about 8am and happened to be looking at the golf house when it suddenly burst into flames. The fire had been smouldering all night and when Sidney Phillips came to work in the morning and opened the door in came the wind and, well, I could hardly believe my eyes!"

Phyllis Jilbert nee Hosking: "I can remember when the pavilion was burnt down. I went up and saw it and picked up a little key to keep in memory of it. The old foundations are still there. The new clubhouse was built on a different spot in little lane and is still standing. It was sold to the Roach's of Trewidden when the Golf Links closed."

Sancreed Golf Pavilion on fire.

Stephen Bennetts recalled that his grandfather, Graham Bennetts, played golf there with the notorious von Ribbentrop who was German Ambassador to Britain in 1937.

Among the many others who played golf at Sancreed were the Simpsons outfitters, Harveys solicitors, N J Hall grocer, and Henry Olds and also the Lord Chancellor, Lord Sankey, plus Sir Justice Gregory and members of the Rothschild family.

Phyllis: "Our sheep grazed on the golf course which was almost half the farm. One day a ram saw his reflection in a big shining new car, charged at it causing damage. Tom Eaves of Lands End Radio often landed his Auster aircraft there when visiting family/friends. John Warren also worked on the greens. When war came in 1939 the Golf Links closed down and the land was ploughed to grow food. The local bus had the destination Golf Links on it and used that route for 20 years after. Many people came up on that bus route and were disappointed, no Golf Links"!

Cyril Lane continued to live there and was employed at Bosistow by Harry Laity and the War Agricultural Committee, doing contract work on farms. He married in 1940. His daughter Margaret was born 1941."

Margaret German nee Lane

"The night I was born the Germans were dropping bombs. The district nurse got there before the doctor. He was sheltering in the hedge. I was premature, weighing only about 4lbs. The doctor pulled the cover back to look at me "Oh she might live". I was fed with a fountain pen filler every hour by Mum and Granny Lane. They were determined to keep me alive. They weren't allowed to pick me up. The district nurse came in every day."

Golf Links sign, James Osborne grandson and Margaret, daughter of Cyril Lane.

CHURCHILL'S SECRET ARMY

In 1941 Margaret's father Cyril Lane became part of Churchill's Secret Army

In 1941 'arms dumps' were hidden all over the country and an underground movement was formed. The Secret Army, trained to halt a Nazi invasion, was the brainchild of Winston Churchill, who feared an invasion was imminent after the evacuation from the beaches of Dunkirk.

They wore Home Guard uniform, had a thorough knowledge of their area, and were specially trained in demolition, unarmed combat, and the art of moving through the countryside unseen and unheard. Every unit had a well-stocked, well-armed bunker hideout from where, if the Germans invaded, they would creep out and sabotage the enemy. This training took place at weekends. During the week they carried on their usual work.

FORMER GOLF PROFESSIONAL'S ESCAPE FROM DEATH
From the *Cornishman* 15 April 1942

"An accident of the most serious nature occurred at Bosistow Farm Porthcurno, on Wednesday afternoon, when Mr. Cyril Lane fell beneath a tractor and disc harrow.

It appears that Mr. Lane, who was driving the tractor, had reason to get off, possibly to make some adjustment. Unfortunately he slipped and the tractor and harrow, continuing their course, went right over him.

Mr. Harry Laity rushed to his assistance and he was taken to the West Cornwall Hospital.

Mr. Lane's escape from death can be described as little less than miraculous, for besides the great weight of the tractor and the sharp, biting teeth of the harrow, a heavy load of broccoli was being carried.

Mr. Lane is very well known in the district. He was the golf professional on the Sancreed course.

Enquiries at the West Cornwall Hospital this (Friday) morning show that Mr. Lane's condition is now quite comfortable."

FOOTNOTE: Apparently he had tripped over a broccoli stump and fallen into a trench between the broccoli banks dragging his coat over his head. Everyone was amazed that he lived, and even more, that after several months in hospital he eventually recovered.

The old Fordsons were so difficult to get into gear that it was not unusual for the driver to step off and adjust the machine while the tractor was on the move.

LITTLE SELLAN

Tommy James: "We came to Little Sellan in 1945 /1946 when father bought it from the Leggo estate in Torquay. It was old fashioned and derelict at that time. We continued as their tenants at Boswarthan and Rose Valley.

The Shorthorns we kept at Boswarthan were brought with us to Little Sellan. I have still got some of the same breeding. We had a heifer once down a mine pit and father couldn't get her out. He was always very friendly with the Richards brothers of Drift with whom he grew up. They brought the *Churchill* (the Richards' homemade mechanical shovel) up to the farm, reversed it to the pit, father went down on the rope, put it around the heifer and they pulled her up. That's the day I rode on the *Churchill*.

Little Sellan. hoeing broccoli, the James family.

Ferguson T20 tractor with Freeman Sanders engine

We had a new Ferguson T20 diesel tractor in Sellan with a 'Freeman Sanders badge on the engine, and father said, "These engines were developed at Trembath Mill by Freeman Sanders."

Sandra and I met at Sancreed Institute. Our son William who works with me lives at Trannack Mill."

SELLAN MILL

History

Beryl Tonkin: "Sellan Mill lies at the very edge of Sancreed Parish near Skimmel Bridge. The Newlyn River, the boundary between Sancreed and Madron Parish, marks the eastern boundary of the property. It appears the Mill existed before the dwelling house, with a stable in which visiting horses were housed. Later, a dwelling house, pigs' houses with cobbled floors, a general store house and a cart-house were built. There was a millstone set in the ground by the garden gate. The Mill was working in 1846 when William Bray was the miller but the mill stopped working around 1880 to 1890. It was two-storied but very little remains except the wheel pit, roughly filled with rocks, a wonderful place for children to play.

Barm

Our neighbour, Johnny Thomas of Little Sellan, said that when the mill was working boys would go to sleep on barley bags, and when the bell rang they would get up and refill the hopper. Mr. Thomas also said that to make barley bread barm was used instead of yeast, and a certain man drank some. He went to bed and swelled up so much he had to be tied down with ropes around the bed, as it was feared he would burst.

Tin Streamers

Around 1885 several tin streamers went up through the valley streaming for tin - there were mines at Tregavara Downs and Carn y Barges nearby - and three caves could be seen the other side of the river. Another cave was lived in by the tin streamers, and was just big enough for someone to stand up in, the front was large enough to fit a door and an upward tunnel let out the smoke of their fire. Into this they had inserted a tin pipe. These tin streamers were considered by the locals to be very rough men, and the local children were told by their parents not to have anything to do with them.

The dwelling house faced east and was very sheltered, though lower fields caught the frost. Sometimes after heavy rain the river would overflow and flood the lower land and I remember my father bringing in the Exmoor pony to higher ground by riding him bareback through the floodwater. Some members of the Wherry family came to Sellan Mill in 1884 and were there until October 1932.

Albert and Katie Elliott (my parents) came there then and they stayed until Michaelmas 1958. Mr. Jim Wherry's, sister and brother-in-law Arthur Bennetts lived there as well, and he was fond of gardening so had a little corner of a meadow for himself. Here, he used to grow flowers, especially Dahlias that were his favourites. When we lived there, this corner was always referred to as Arthur's garden. At the northern end of our five and a quarter acres, just across the river, once stood a tucking mill, Vellandruchia. Only a slight unevenness of ground and a hedged lane leading up to the later house showed a former settlement. Father was returning to the house one evening and told us when he came indoors that he had seen a woman at the edge of the yard near the woodshed. Why he didn't challenge her, or why we girls didn't go out to see where she went I don't know, thinking back she was probably a ghost!"

DISASTER AS THRESHING ENGINE EXPLODES

Albert Elliott, mentioned above, was 11 years old in 1917 when, at his home farm Banns, St Buryan the boiler of a threshing machine exploded killing John Prisk of Cockwells, Ludgvan and injuring John Angwin, and a soldier from the depot at Bodmin.

Threshing day had begun as usual with the farmer, Albert E. Elliott (grandfather of Beryl Tonkin of Newlyn, and her sister Ruby Martin) allocating the men their jobs. At 1.00 pm something went wrong with the belt the machine was stopped and this was adjusted, and the engine man was in the act of bringing the piston back to centre in order to start the machine again when the engine exploded.

So great was the force of the explosion that the shell of the boiler, the engine and the firebox were lifted more than 10ft off the ground and thrown to the further side of the threshing machine where they were hanging over the side on to the straw-lifter. John Prisk, the engine-man was killed instantly.

John Angwin's injuries were not very serious, but with pain and shock he ran to his home at St.Buryan, about a mile away. He was on the rick at the time of the accident and received scalds.

The soldier was more seriously scalded and was taken to West Cornwall Infirmary.

Albert E. Elliott, the farmer, said when the explosion occurred he was between the machine and the corn rick. The force threw him off his feet and carried him the length of the machine.

SELLAN MILL

Tom Paynter & Ann Dakin

In the early 1960s Tom Paynter and his sister Mrs Ann Dakin retired to Sellan Mill.

Their father Commander Hugh Paynter had been commissioned to secretly deliver a cruiser, the Kasuga, to Japan in January 1904 from Genoa in Italy. His brother Colonel Paynter was with him as gunner and to impose discipline, for the crew were a motley crowd of men picked up from the docks. They were flying a Japanese flag at a time when Japan was at war with Russia, (Britain feared Russian expansion and were secretly allied with Japan). The Emperor of Japan conferred on Hugh the Order of the Rising Sun.

Hugh, who died in 1934, married Beatrice Louisa Barkworth of Oxted in Surrey in1890 who in the First War was in charge of the forces hospital at Heligan, in Cornwall. Hugh and Beatrice had three children:

1) **Ann**, born 1892 was a lifelong supporter of the Scout and Guide movement, a talented horsewoman and rider. She married Capt. Geoffrey Dakin of, Surrey who died in 1931.

She formed a troop of about 30 guides at St Buryan in 1938 and played violin in the Penzance Orchestra after coming to live in Lamorna, where she had Trevellen built for her. This was a smallholding and she kept goats.

She was childless and adopted a son Paul aged 10 in 1947. She died in 1980. Both she and her sister Donnett had been presented at court.

2) **Donnett**, (born 1894) in the First World War drove an ambulance in France for three years. After the war she became a competent musician. She died in 1921 aged 27.

3) **Tom** was born in1901 at Rye. From a boy he composed and performed music in public. The Penzance Orchestral Society performed his composition of 'The Newlyn Suite' in 1946 at St John's Hall. He was a Commando Major and was in the Lovat Scouts in Canada during the Second World War. He died at Sellan Mill, Sancreed in 1976.

SELLAN VEOR

Sellan has been the home of the Wherry family for almost 120 years.

Nicholas Wherry, born at Cardinham in 1839, a gardener, married Elizabeth Calf of St Austell.

Their sons, William and James, were born at St.Austell in 1867 and 1869; Stephen was possibly born at Camborne around 1870, Edith at Towednack in 1875 and Nicholas junior at Ludgvan in 1880. There was also Louie and Bessie. Later, Nicholas junior emigrated to Australia.

The Wherry family came to Sellan in1884. In the 1891 census Nicholas and his family, including his son William, were at Sellan Mill. Nicholas was market gardening.

William married Dorcas Chellew from Boscawenoon and the 1901 census St Buryan showed them with their son, Henry, aged 4 and a daughter Grace aged 2 (born Sancreed), and Percy aged 1 (born at Chycandria St Buryan).

William farmed for a while as tenant at Trannack, Sancreed. At the end of his first year his landlord said to him "Have you made a profit this year William?" "Yes, why did you ask?" "Because if you hadn't I'd give you the fertiliser because I'm not going to see my farm go without".

By 1914 William was farming Sellan Veor, which he, by then, owned.

Nicholas died in 1913 and his brother, James, took his place as market gardener at Sellan Mill. James died in 1935. His son Henry married Mabel Hosken and was farming at Brane.

Henry's brother, Percy Wherry, farmed Sellan Veor in the 1930s, followed by his son, Leslie, who married in 1950. Leslie's son Stephen and wife Clare now farm there.

Between SellanVeor and Treganhoe Farm there was a **STAMPS** in the river leading to the reservoir. Here the tin ore would be brought from Carn-e-barges, the tin mine on the wasteland on the other side of the farm, to be crushed and washed.

About three acres of SellanVeor Farm were lost in Drift Reservoir, as were parts of two other farms, Codna Coath, and Nanquitho.

Most of the land remaining has now become part of Sellan Veor.

NANQUITHO

Willie Wallis, a local preacher in the St Just circuit, farmed at Nanquitho for many years. His granddaughter Sheila Hosking lives at St Buryan.

After the war, Philip John Pengelly farmed part time at Nanquitho. He helped a Paul farmer milk forty cows and then came home to milk his own eight.

Philip, his wife, and daughter Margaret moved to nearby Codna Coath in the early 1950s.

TREGANHOE

The James family first moved to Treganhoe around 1923 – William Wearne James, his wife Annie (nee Berryman of Porthmeor, Zennor), their young sons Wearne & Dennis (lived in Treganhoe house), William Wearne's parents, William Edward & Margaret James, along with his Uncle, William Hocking Wearne & his widowed aunt, Mary Ann Glasson (lived in Treganhoe Farmhouse). The family moved from Trelean & Lanuthnoe in St Erth, from where they drove their livestock all the way from St Erth to Sancreed. With William & Annie also came Violet Angove, who they had taken into their family as a young girl to help with domestic chores. Later, after Violet had married Tom Courtney, the back kitchen of the big house was converted into their own living quarters, where they lived until moving out to Drift. Violet always referred to Mrs James affectionately as 'mother'.

Mrs Annie James offered Bed & Breakfast at Treganhoe, and her many visitors included actor John Mills, whose sister was staying down at Stamps at that time. Annie's daughter-in-law, Catherine continued the Bed, Breakfast & Evening meal business at Treganhoe, in the farmhouse, with some families returning 10 years consecutively!

When evacuees arrived at Sancreed during the Second World War, the vicar was involved in assigning them to the various households of the parish. He came up to Mrs Annie James and remarked that as she had a big house she could take four evacuees; Mrs James was quick to point out that the vicarage was a good size too, and that she would take her four evacuees once the vicar had taken his four! This must have made the vicar reassess the situation, as the James family ended up with two evacuees! The evacuees, Dennis and Paul Gaston, were made very welcome at Treganhoe, and Dennis, who stayed on at Treganhoe until he was about 18, (known as Fred, so as not to get confused with Dennis James) is still in touch with the James family, and visits Treganhoe whenever he returns 'home' from Australia, where he now lives.

William Wearne James (Wearne) married Joyce Eddy and moved to Boswarthen and later to Sellan. In 1947, Dennis Berryman James married Catherine Maud Trewern of Trewoofe, Lamorna. Her father, John Henry, was the chauffeur to Colonel Paynter of Boskenna, before he took over the farm at Trewoofe, after spending World War 1 as an ambulance driver in France. Dennis and Catherine had two children, Jennifer and Ivor who attended Sancreed School, before moving on to Heamoor School (where Jennifer became Head Girl). Both Jennifer & Ivor have fond memories of their time at Sancreed School.

William Wearne James died on October 13th 1943, aged 51. His coffin was draped with the Union Jack flag, as a mark of respect for his role in the First World War. Wearne and Dennis were both members of the Home Guard.

After their father died, Treganhoe was run by Dennis and his mother, Annie. When Dennis's son Ivor left school, he came home to Treganhoe, to work alongside his father, Dennis.

In 1963 some of Treganhoe's land was purchased to make way for Drift Reservoir; Mrs Annie James bought a grandfather clock from one of the ladies whose cottage was part of the land due to be flooded – the clock was duly named after the lady and 'Martha' stood proudly for many years, admired by successive generations.

Sancreed Feast was always a very special day at Treganhoe – Mrs Annie James and her daughter-in-law, Catherine, would both lay on fine spreads – Catherine's mother, Maud, had been a Thomas from Lanyon before she married John Henry Trewern, a family that loved a get-together, so Sancreed Feast saw a lively gathering of the James, Berrymans, Trewerns and Thomases at Treganhoe, with much laughter and catching up on all the local news.

Dennis and Catherine's daughter, Jennifer, married John Kitto of Leedstown in 1968, whilst their son, Ivor, married Susan Semmens in 1977, at Sennen Church. John and Jennifer moved to Bodilly Vean, Wendron, and had three sons – James, Julian and Jeffrey. Ivor and Susan stayed at Treganhoe, and had a son, Mark and a daughter, Alison. Mark became a keen farmer and married Adele Jewell, whilst Alison became a legal executive. Ivor and Mark continue to farm Treganhoe".

TRERICE

My memories of potato harvesting from 1916 to 1982

Leonard Hosken: I left school in 1915, too late for the potato season. My first memory of helping was in 1916. We first started digging with shovels we got a load that day and loaded them in the cart in the evening. These first earlies were packed in hampers with straw laced over the top to protect them in transport. Later, hessian sacks were used. After breakfast I took them to railway sidings at Ponsandane.

Lifting all these potatoes by shovels was a slow job. As time went on most farmers had the breast of their single ploughs removed and a different shape fitted - this lifted the row of potatoes leaving the stems facing upward, we then had to shake the potatoes from the stems, dig the furrow through and pick up the potatoes.

At the beginning of the 1939 war we had to plant a larger acreage and a new digger was available. Drawn by horses this lifted and separated potatoes from stems and we could pick up the potatoes, which were scattered over the ground. This was a little easier than digging, but still tedious and hard on the back from bending.

The next machine was drawn by a big tractor which lifted the rows one at a time and they caught on an elevator by the platform manned by five or six men who picked out any earth or stones, the potatoes then went over another channel to the front of the tractor where two more men caught them in bags, weighed and tied them to be unloaded at the end of the row. By this method fifteen or twenty tons, could be harvested in one day. Motor transport was now available so they could be loaded on the lorry direct from the field.

Now I am over eighty and have just watched a machine digging but instead of bagging, the crop goes into a hopper which is tipped at the end of the rows to a waiting trailer which again is taken to a lorry and tipped in a small elevator to be loaded loose onto a lorry and taken to a factory for making potato crisps. Two of these twenty-ton lorries were filled in one day."

Morley Hosken

"Although my father and his parents came to Trerice from St Levan in the 1920s following my grandfather's purchase of the farm, the Hosken family were already established in Sancreed. My great-grandfather had farmed at Bosence for a number of years and my father and his sister were born at Ennestreven. My grandfather Nicholas White Hosken was the youngest of the 21 children of John T Hosken whose grave is in the old cemetery below Sancreed church. My parents were married in 1925 and my sister Avis and I were born at Trerice and attended the Church of England school in the village.

In those days there were none of the services which we take for granted today and the school boys were expected to fetch the water each day from the village pump situated outside the farmhouse at Glebe.

At that time Glebe was farmed by Mr James Stevens, the son of James Stevens whose diary was published many years after his death.

Life must have been very full for Mr Stevens in those years and James junior was his only son. I can remember most of the sisters quite well, particularly Mabel the youngest who married my great uncle Bert Reynolds. I believe that several of the Stevens reached a great age, James died aged 93 and Mabel aged 95.

ACV 123

I remember the first motor car that my father owned, a soft top vehicle with what was known as a dickie seat at the rear. My sister and I were perched in this precarious position when visiting our various relatives, no seat belts for us. Later on my father bought a new Austin 7 quite a smart little car with the registration number ACV 123. I wonder what that number would be worth today?

The river which forms the boundary between Trerice and Sellan and ends at the reservoir at Drift flows beneath the road at Trerice Bridge. On this spot were 2 cottages one of these was home to a wonderful old couple called Mr and Mrs Richard Kent who my sister and I always thought of as grandparents. They lived very modestly but were apparently quite content and frequently bought little gifts of sweets for my sister and me. Dick, as everyone called him could always be relied upon to give a hand on the farm.

Threshing Day

I remember when Dick Lanyon from Rospeath brought his steam engine and threshing machine to Trerice. I spent most of the day hauling churns of water for the traction engine from the well at the bottom of the hill. Threshing was always exciting for the children but I do not think my mother shared our enthusiasm, the machine operators would spend the night here before the day of threshing to enable them to get up early to stoke up the engine, and as we had no bathroom or facilities such as hot and cold running water there were a lot of grubby sheets to wash.

Horse on pub-crawl.

Mr and Mrs Phillips were a wonderful old couple who had a family of 3 boys and a girl, I recall one of the sons telling me of the time when his father, (who had a fruit and vegetable business and travelled around the Pendeen, Trewellard and St Just area) was unwell and asked his son to drive the horse and wagon around to serve all his customers. The story he related was that the journey took much longer than he imagined as the horse persisted in stopping at every public house, and in that area there were quite a few!

After my father retired and Eira and I were married with a young family, I had to modernize and expand the milking herd from 19 in my father's time to a 40 cow milking parlour but on the acreage available to us, even with family labour, the future looked uncertain, so I decided to disperse our dairy herd and concentrate on my herd of pedigree Landrace pigs.

One of the Hosking brothers, Jack shared my enthusiasm for pig breeding and was with me when I exhibited or judged at shows and sales around the country. Sadly all the Sellan Boys have now passed away but I have very fond memories of them all and of our times together in the days both before, during and after the last war and I feel fortunate to have lived to see our children and our grandchildren grow up and still live in the same district in which the Hosken family lived for so many generations."

Morley's Sancreed Pigs.

153

SANCREED VILLAGE AGAIN

The Rodda family

We have travelled clockwise around the parish and are back again near Sancreed village.

Now travelling back in time two and a half centuries we meet the Rodda family, the three brothers who were John Wesley's travelling preachers.

Richard Rodda, Wesleys Preacher.

Richard Rodda
Richard Rodda was born into a poor family in Sancreed, Cornwall in 1743.

"Now hark 'ee! I wean't have none of 'ee havin'' nawthen' to do with these 'ere Methodies." That was the way old Nicholas Rodda talked to his family down in Sancreed in those far off days when John Wesley himself was riding round the county. There were ten children in that home, and Honour the eldest, despite her father's strict orders, one day went to a Methodist service. Later her mother went too, and they both joined the little Methodist Society. After a while they won over old Mr. Rodda, and there were regular services conducted in their house by the despised 'Methodies'.

One of the Rodda boys, Richard by name, had a narrow escape from death when galloping on a horse. It made him take a much more serious view of life. He, too, became a Methodist; in fact he entered into full membership at a memorable meeting at Newlyn, when John Wesley himself called the roll of new members. Richard Rodda, a tin-miner was at one point press-ganged into the Navy but was released through the good offices of a Quaker friend.

In a letter to John Wesley he wrote, *"Some time after, I had another proof of God's mercy and goodness. I was one day standing on what we call in Cornwall a borough of attle which filled an old tin-pit, and stood a considerable height from the surface of the earth. While I was standing on its top, it sunk in an instant under my feet; and I literally went down quick into the pit. The attle immediately followed me, and covered my head; but I went down till I came where a miner was working, He was greatly surprised to see me. If I had been retarded in my passage, I must have been inevitably suffocated. I received no damage."*

Rodda began to preach in 1769. Hearing that John Wesley wanted a regular preacher for the Glamorganshire Circuit, he volunteered and was accepted. Out of his own money he bought a horse, and started into what he called his "round".

In 1770, as minister of the Brecon Methodist Circuit he visited Hereford and decided to preach out of doors by St Nicholas Church. A man made an attempt to throw a pail of milk over him. Another man called Bacon gathered dirt from the kennel and threw it in his face causing him to stop. Richard Rodda went to the local Justice of the Peace's house to have the man punished under the 1689 Act of Toleration. The JP was loathe to arrest him as he had a wife and children and Rev. Rodda said that he did not want him arrested just warned against making a disturbance again. After that he was able to preach in peace.

He was present when John Wesley died in1791.

Richard was a man of great physical strength. His active circuit ministry of thirty-three years was exercised mainly in the south and west and was characterised by great hardship. He became old before his time. Exposure again and again to wet and cold in Cornwall, in Oxfordshire and elsewhere, led to his having to retire from the active work, and he spent his last days in London, where he was often seen at Wesley's Chapel, City Road. He was buried there when he died in 1815.

A descendant David Dearlove lives in Penzance.

The Rodda family - Martin Rodda b 1737

Though some of the English preachers had returned to England, and war between America and England was now imminent, Wesley sent out recruits to the small group of preachers, for he believed that Methodism was now a permanent fact in the moral destiny of the New World, and should be supported for the future. Accordingly in 1774 Martin Rodda was sent.

Martin Rodda had travelled about twelve years before his departure for America. He remained there less than three years, and is accused of having circulated over his circuit, in Delaware, the royal proclamation against the American patriots. Much of that fierce persecution which his brethren in the ministry suffered after his departure was the consequence of his indiscretion. He had to flee from the country, and made his escape, by the aid of slaves, to the British fleet, whence he was conveyed to Philadelphia, then in possession of the English army, and thence to England.

The Rodda Family – Thomas Rodda b1748

Thomas Rodda was the least well known of the three Rodda preachers from Sancreed.

The Rodda Family – William Rodda was the father of Ann Johns

Ann Johns (1773-1860) daughter of William was a devoted and lifelong Anglican. She married Thomas Johns who divided his time between his liquor establishments at Roscoff in Brittany and Sennen and St Buryan in Cornwall. Perhaps his murder on the road between his Cornish houses accentuated his reputation but he was said to have been eminently pious. Ann was sixteen when John Wesley was last in St Just and in her old age she loved to talk of him. What seems odd in her whose husband had been a gentleman (i.e. a smuggler and an agent), was that she recommended to all, the drinking of nettle tea. John Wesley had told her that nettle tea was a pharmacopoeia in itself.

In this book you have travelled the parish from end to end.
You have met the people, some of whom may be on your family tree.

You have travelled round the parish visiting familiar places and some of which
you may never have heard before.

You have learned of past events, some going back hundreds of years and some
more recent ones. Each place has a story to tell. I hope that sharing in their lives
will have been an interesting experience to store away in your memories.

If you have enjoyed reading this book
you may also like to read our other title in this series,
PEOPLE & PLACES IN PAUL PARISH including Mousehole & Newlyn

ACKNOWLEDGEMENTS and THANKS
My thanks go to so many people who have shown interest and helped with
this book. Here are some of them.

Dream Princess by Elizabeth Forbes.
Painting by permission of the Trustees of the Royal Institution of Cornwall
Riding School photos   Vanessa Oates
Margo Maeckelberghe with her painting   David and Jill Try.
Flying tractor   Eamonn & Foncene Cocking
Sheila Hicks   Jill Leiworthy,
Ponies at Ennestreven   painting by Sarah Carter
Early milk vans & factory   Trevor & Michael Richards
Bird in Hand & others   Glyn Richards
Prince Charles   Norman Hosking
Sancreed school 1953-56   Michael Richards
My Wedding Day   Norah Pearce
Sancreed school late 1950s   Penny Thomas
Newbridge school, Botrea, Botrea Mine, rocket store, Bog Inn & others   Ron Prowse
Boswens & family picture   John Trewern
Wesleys plane & thresher   Rodney Hutchings
Dairy Princess   Anita George
Chycoll   David Ceredig-Evans
Doris, Jack Clarice, & Everett White and family   Ivy Harris
Will Tregear   Reg Watkiss
Family picture   Arnold Oates
Pigs   Morley Hosken,
Joan   Mick Angwin,
Wesley's veterans   Cedric Appleby
Pengelly's Tregonebris   George Rich

Francis Angwin
Jan Bird
Stephen Bennetts
Dorothy & Malcolm Bishop
& Penny Bottrell
Ken & Jean Bottrell
Jack & Alice Branwell
Jenny Bray
Alan Buckley
Ken & Joyce Cargeeg
Robin Menneer
Sandra Cox
Dr R Dyke
Keith Eddy
Cyril & Robert Eddy
Gladys Gendall
Margaret & David German
Betty Grey
Eileen Harvey
Audrey & Leonard Harvey
Barbara Hattam
Mark Hattam
Justus Hattam
Matthew Hill
Vivienne Hocking
James Hosking, Sandra & Susan
Kathleen & Alan Hosking
Clarence & Muriel Hosken
Marion Hosking
Rodney Hutchings
Chris & Angela James
William James
Tommy & Sandra James
Monica James
Mr & Mrs James
Phyllis Jilbert
Beverley Kendall
Barbara Lever
James Kitto

Ron Lyon
Peter & Jo Alexander Marrack
Michael Matthews
Jo Mattingly
Desmond Nicholls
Hilda Nicholls
Hedley & Doreen Nicholls
Miss North
Alfred Olds
Jennifer Paling
Joe Pengelly
John & William Pengelly
Barry Reynolds
Lloyd Reynolds
Dr Eric Richards
John Richards
Wendy Richards
Bob Rogers
Melville, Donald, Leslie, & Geoff Rowe
Terry Shorland
Emma Slack nee Glossop
Rose Smith
William John & DianeThomas
Beryl & Raymond Tonkin
Winifred Treleven
Sidney Trembath
Margaret Trembath
Edith Try
Mary Waters
Reg Watkiss
Eileen Wherry
Melville & Trevor Wherry
Stephen & Clare Wherry
Ken Williams
Phillip Williams
Ken Wood
Jill Woodhead
Fiona Young

The Cornishman, Western Morning News, West Britain, The Morrab Gardens Library and The Public Library, Penzance, Cornwall Records Office, The Courtney Library, Cornwall Family History Society, and Cornish Local Studies Library, West Penwith Resources, also thanks to many others who have provided information.

A special thanks also to three people
Alison Bevan for her excellent "Foreword"for this book,
Nancy Wallis and Jean White for editing, advice and encouragement.

BIBLIOGRAPHY

John Miller – Leave tomorrow behind

J W Scobell Armstrong – Yesterday

D B Barton – A history of tin mining & smelting in Cornwall

Peter Joseph – Mining accidents in the St Just District 1831 – 1914

W Bottrell – Legends and Hearthside Stories of West Cornwall

Kathleen Hawke – Bird In Hand

James Stevens – A Cornish Farmer's Diary

Rodney Lyon, ex Grand Bard - Plan-an-gwarry

Rie M Fletcher & Joan R fortes – Hicks Family

Desmond Nicholls – copy of Catchall Dairy Company Minutes

Capt. John RN & Peter Alexander-Marrack - The Marracks of Tregonebris

Jim Remphrey – End to End

Ivy Harris copy of Edward Thomas White's Diary

Richard G Grylls – Branwell & Bramble a brief history of a West Cornwall Clan

Rev. John Pearce –The Wesleys in Cornwall